R. R. STATION

CRUMWOLD

F. W. VANDERBILT MANSION

TOWN HALL

JAMES ROOSEVELT LIBRARY

HYDE PARK

ROUTE 9

POST OFFICE

ST. JAMES CHURCH

SITE OF FIRST BARD HOUSE

ELEMENTARY SCHOOL

EWBOLD HOUSE

TWO 18th CENTURY DUTCH HOUSES

ST. JAMES CHAPEL

EAST PARK ROAD

DICKINSON MILL

EAST PARK

CRUM ELBOW CREEK

BENJAMIN HAVILAND FARM

SITE OF UNION CORNERS RACE TRACK

FRANKLIN D. ROOSEVELT HIGH SCHOOL

VAL-KILL FARMS

PICTORIAL MAP
of
HYDE PARK

From Rosedale to St. James Church is 3.3 miles. From the Franklin D. Roosevelt Library to Top Cottage is 3 miles.

Franklin Roosevelt
at Hyde Park

Franklin Roosevelt
at Hyde Park

Documented Drawings and Text

by

OLIN DOWS

AMERICAN ARTISTS GROUP, *inc.* NEW YORK

29875

TO

MY MOTHER

Roosevelt.

ACKNOWLEDGMENTS

My debt to most of those persons whose names appear on the following pages—for their letters, the stories they have told me, the loans of family documents and photographs, or permission to make drawings of places and objects in their possession—is obvious. I shall not repeat their names here, but they can see how valuable their help has been to me; I thank them for it.

George Palmer and Frederick Rath, of the National Park Service, have been most helpful, by giving me easy access to the house and grounds of this National Historic Site. Frederick Shipman, former director of the Franklin D. Roosevelt Library, Martin P. Claussen, acting director, and Herman Kahn, the present director, have been good enough to give me permission to make drawings of objects in the Library, as well as to reproduce and quote from documents. To every individual on the Roosevelt place, and to the entire staff of the Library, go my thanks for their courtesy and help during the not inconsiderable time these drawings have been in the making. Henry J. Toombs has generously allowed me to reproduce Mr. Roosevelt's original sketch of Top Cottage, which is in his possession. The Reverend Gordon Kidd has made it easy for me to draw in St. James Church. Harry Wickey's careful reading of the final manuscript has added to its clarity.

The following authors and publishers have very kindly permitted me to quote from the following publications: "Franklin D. Roosevelt" by Ernest K. Lindley, published by The Bobbs-Merrill Company, Inc.; "This Is My Story" by Eleanor Roosevelt, published by Harper Brothers; also from Eleanor Roosevelt's column "My Day" released through the United Feature Syndicate, "F.D.R. Early Letters" edited by Elliott Roosevelt, published by Duell, Sloane & Pearce; "My Boy Franklin" as told by Sara Delano Roosevelt to Isabel Leighton and Gabrielle Forbush, published by Richard R. Smith, Inc.; "Gracious Lady" by Rita Halle

Kleeman, published by D. Appleton-Century Co., for the material acknowledged in the text and all the quotations from Mrs. James Roosevelt's diary; "Young Franklin Roosevelt" by Rita Halle Kleeman, published by Julian Messner, "The Roosevelt I Knew" by Frances Perkins, published by Viking Press; "Starling of the White House" by Thomas Sugrue, published by Simon & Schuster, "Roosevelt and Hopkins" by Robert E. Sherwood, published by Harper Brothers, "The New Republic," April 15, 1946, articles by Mrs. Charles Hamlin, and Archibald MacLeish.

There are three friends to whom I owe a special debt: Margaret L. Suckley, who has not only been a continual source of ideas and information, as well as an invaluable helper in her capacity as one of the archivists of the Franklin D. Roosevelt Library, but also has most generously let me use her notes and quote directly from her unpublished diary; Archibald MacLeish, whose constructive criticism on the writing has enhanced materially the final product; and Samuel Golden, whose idea the book was; his intelligent comments on the drawings and the text and his infectious enthusiasm have added to my pleasure in its execution.

INTRODUCTION

I am a painter who has lived most of my life in Rhinebeck, New York. Our place is eight miles north of the Roosevelts' at Hyde Park. I knew Mr. Roosevelt as a family friend throughout my childhood. His children, Anna and James, came to the dancing class that met at our house. Our families had been neighbors on the Hudson River for several generations before that, and, like most of the old Valley families, have ancestors in common.

Country life in our part of the Hudson Valley has changed singularly little from the time of my grandfather and my mother, who was F.D.R.'s contemporary, to the days of my own childhood. Only after the first World War did the full impact of our mechanized society, the telephone, the motor car, chain stores, heavy traffic on concrete roads, start transforming us from a country to a suburban community.

This is a picture book about the Valley as I remember it and about the Roosevelts—particularly about the President. But I must warn you that it is a picture book accompanied by thoroughly informal notes. I have drawn certain objects because they seemed to me to have a reference personal to Mr. Roosevelt. I have drawn none because they were important objects (though some of them were that too). The pictures and the notes sometimes suggest Mr. Roosevelt's character, sometimes the way he lived. They are neither comprehensive nor exhaustive. They are not history, though history may remember some of them.

The drawings were finished, in most cases, before the notes were assembled. They follow a rough chronology, but the dates of diaries, letters, and speeches move back and forth. This record has grown from talks with F.D.R., his family and neighbors, from thumbing through old albums, and from memories. Do not expect it to give you new, startling, or dramatic facts. If it helps you to understand the county and the life in which the President grew up, it will have served its purpose. I think Mr. Roosevelt would have enjoyed this record. He was very conscious of his Hyde Park background.

That background was twofold: It was one of place—our Hudson River landscape, and one of time—the long line of men and women reaching back to the settlement of the Valley. Besides my wish to show Franklin Roosevelt's own background, I hope that these drawings will evoke, as well, the memories of all country-bred men and women—their pets, their games, in winter their coasting down long, unencumbered hills; in summer their fishing and boating; their adventures in the woods with its furry, feathered, or scaly inhabitants; the first dog-tooth violets and skunk cabbages; the red lizard on the moss after a summer shower; the treasure chest in the dark attic; the birds watched over or robbed; the occasional trip to the village, with the treat of ice cream; the yearly visit to the circus, the Decoration Day parade. The sights and sounds and smells that accompany these memories helped to make the great man's background—one in which many of us have shared.

It may increase your enjoyment of the pictures which follow if I tell you a few facts about this county of ours. The actual country concerned is an oblong piece of flat, rolling and wooded farm land, lying on the east bank of the Hudson River. It starts at Fishkill, about fifty-five miles north of New York

City, and extends forty miles along the river. It stretches inland twenty-five miles. The River is a leading character in this narrative; even when it doesn't appear in a drawing, it is still very much present. Since the earliest days it has been an integral part of our life. The Hudson, and the Catskill Mountains in the background, make our landscape distinctive.

At first there was an Indian trail from New Amsterdam, as New York City was then called, to Fort Orange, later called Albany. It ran parallel to the Hudson, and inland sometimes as much as three miles. Later this became the Post Road. Now it is Route 9. The Hudson River Railroad, now the New York Central, was constructed to follow the river's edge. It was built northward from New York City and southward from Albany. The two sections joined below Hyde Park in 1850.

Most of the country places I discuss in the notes which follow lie between Route 9 and the River. You will find their relative positions clearly shown on the maps which make the end papers of this book. Although we go twenty-five miles north of Hyde Park village in one picture, and almost the same distance south and across the river to Newburgh in another, the body of this record lies in that narrow strip.

The families which live on the river estates are called locally "the River families." Many of them, including the Roosevelts and ourselves, are descendants of the Beekmans and the Livingstons. These two families were among the forty which, between 1685 and 1781, received a dozen patents from the British Crown for the land which is now Dutchess County. About half of these original land grants went to Dutchmen, like the Beekmans, the others to Englishmen, like the Livingstons. The grants were preceded by deeds of purchase from the Indians, who were, and continued to be, friendly.

Most of the early patentees lived abroad or in New York City. They were absentee landlords who allotted tracts of the still unsettled country to the men and women who actually cleared the land and cultivated it. When these settlers had money they bought the land outright, and thus became freeholders. Only freeholders could vote. Most of the settlers, however, could not pay cash. They did not own the land they worked, but paid to the patentee rent in kind, usually in wheat. During the first two decades of the Eighteenth-century fewer than a third of the county population were freeholders. By the middle of the century, however, the population had almost quadrupled, and the feudal system of land tenure became increasingly unpopular. What has been called the "Rent War" started in 1766 north of us, in Columbia County. It was a symptom of the discontent that was one of the causes contributing to the War of the Revolution.

Unlike some of the landowners and families of wealth and position, the Beekman-Livingston clan were on the right side, that of the numerical majority, for about two-thirds of the population signed the Revolutionary pledge. Many of the non-signing third, however, owned much of the wealth, and considered themselves the "best people." Even the distinguished, public-spirited and able Dr. John Bard of Hyde Park was a Tory. So was his son Samuel.

One of the first Beekmans, who lived in Kingston, across the river from Rhinebeck, had an only daughter, Margaret. She married Robert R. Livingston. This union joined two of the great original land grants. Of their ten surviving children, all were men and women active in the service of the United States — from the oldest son, Robert R., the Chancellor, to the youngest, Edward, of Louisiana Purchase fame; so were their sons-in-law, Generals Richard Montgomery and John Armstrong, Thomas Tillotson, who was Surgeon General of Washington's Northern armies, Freeborn Garretson, Methodist circuit rider, and Morgan Lewis, Governor of New York. The home of Governor Lewis, in Staatsburg, is now a state museum and park. It is the most southerly of the Livingston daughters' country places. There are others throughout the county. Many of the family names are also to be found on the memorial plaques in St. James Church at Hyde Park, and other old churches in our community. Descendants of these families still live on some of the River estates.

As President Roosevelt pointed out, he was descended on his mother's side from the Beekmans and ". . . on the Roosevelt side my great-great-grand-father lived in Rhinebeck for some time during the Revolution and was not only a member of the State Senate, as his great-great-grandson was, but also a member of the Dutchess County militia." This was Isaac Roosevelt.

I lay such stress on this part of our county background because I believe the example of these people exerted a real pull on F.D.R.'s personality. He was proud that his ancestors had been a part of the American Revolutionary tradition. Both his father, James Roosevelt, and his mother, Sara Delano, were undoubtedly conscious of the part their families had played in our country's growth. I suspect that the emphasis was more on public service than on the Revolutionary aspects of the tradition.

Mr. and Mrs. James Roosevelt's family life was in many ways closer to that of the early Nineteenth-century than it was to the hectic period of industrial expansion of the Eighteen-eighties. They lived in great comfort and with a certain style, but without ostentation. They traveled much, but they had deep roots in their community. They "belonged."

This concrete sense of "belonging" colored F.D.R.'s outlook. Because he was able to identify himself so closely with his own community, he was able later to get close to other communities. When he spoke of these things, it was with the understanding of traditions, not only intellectually grasped but slowly absorbed from growing up in their midst. From his relations with his neighbors he knew that a national, even a world problem, always came down to a personal problem. He tells us that when writing his fireside chat on the banking crisis he was trying to make these problems clear to his old friends and neighbors, to individuals in Dutchess County. It was because Mr. Roosevelt thought in terms of the individual that each listener felt he was being spoken to individually. Yet Mr. Roosevelt never "talked down." And that too he may have learned within the dignity of this rural community.

"Glenburn"
Rhinebeck, New York,
August 14, 1948.

The Roosevelt Family Bible, on which F.D.R. took the oath of office twice as Governor and four times as President. (The Bible was published at Amsterdam by Marcus Doornick in 1686, and has been handed down through generations of Roosevelts, probably from Jacobus, the President's great-great-great grandfather.)

*　　*　　*

"I am very busy with a thesis for History 10 on the 'Roosevelts in New Amsterdam.' I have been in the library constantly looking up old records, but nothing much is to be found. Do please copy for me all the extracts in our old Dutch Bible and send them to me . . . I must have them as soon as possible as my notes must be in in a week." Letter from F.D.R. to his mother, Cambridge, Massachusetts, November 18, 1901.

Franklin Roosevelt
at Hyde Park

"Darling Son: Hyde Park, Sunday night, May 8, 1932

"Just 51 years yesterday, the 7th, I came to visit and I moved up yesterday! If I had not come then, I should now be 'old Miss Delano' after a rather sad life!"

*   *   *

May 11, 1932

". . . In writing you I said 51 years. It is really 52 since I came to visit in May. I am not famous as a mathematician."

From letters by Sara Delano Roosevelt to F.D.R.

Thus Mrs. Roosevelt wrote to her son then the Governor of New York, about her first visit to Hyde Park in 1880. She had met James Roosevelt at Theodore Roosevelt's home in New York City when she was twenty-six and he was a widower twice her age and an old friend of her father. The family soon realized, however, that these visits by James Roosevelt to Warren Delano and his household were the beginning of an energetic courtship of his daughter Sara.

Alden Hatch quotes Warren Delano as saying, "Mr. Roosevelt is the first person who has made me realize that a Democrat can be a gentleman."

A visit by Sara Delano to James Roosevelt's Hyde Park country place "Springwood" was quite a normal step in the growing friendship between the two families. On May 7, 1880, Mr. Roosevelt asked "Miss Sallie" to arrange the roses for the luncheon table. From among the many vases in the pantry she chose a low, blue bowl of oriental design; the bowl still stands on the dining-room table at "Springwood."

GETTING READY FOR THE NEW BABY; BASSINET NOW IN THE LIBRARY.

3

MRS. JAMES ROOSEVELT'S ROOM, IN WHICH
FRANKLIN WAS BORN ON JANUARY 30, 1882.

"He was born right here in this house, of course — one never went to hospitals in those days . . . but I am old-fashioned enough to think it's nicer for a baby to be born in his own house. I've passed the door of that sunny, up-stairs room many hundreds of times in my long life and, oh! so often I've remembered that there my son first saw the light of day!"

From "My Boy Franklin"

FIRST BABY SHOES, WORN BY FRANKLIN FROM JULY THROUGH OCTOBER, 1882.

THE WESTERN UNION TELEGRAPH COMPANY.

ALL MESSAGES TAKEN BY THIS COMPANY SUBJECT TO THE FOLLOWING TERMS:

To guard against mistakes or delays, the sender of a message should order it REPEATED; that is, telegraphed back to the originating office for comparison. For this, one half the regular rate is charged in addition. It is agreed between the sender of the following message and this Company, that said Company shall not be liable for mistakes or delays in the transmission or delivery, or for non-delivery, of any UNREPEATED message, whether happening by negligence of its servants or otherwise, beyond the amount received for sending the same; nor for mistakes or delays in the transmission or delivery, or for non-delivery of any REPEATED message beyond fifty times the sum received for sending the same, unless specially insured; nor in any case for delays arising from unavoidable interruption in the working of its lines, or for errors in cipher or obscure messages. And this Company is hereby made the agent of the sender, without liability, to forward any message over the lines of any other Company when necessary to reach its destination. Correctness in the transmission of messages to any point on the lines of this Company can be

INSURED by contract in writing, stating agreed amount of risk, and payment of premium thereon at the following rates, in addition to the usual charge for repeated messages, viz.: one per cent. for any distance not exceeding 1,000 miles, and two per cent. for any greater distance. No employee of the Company is authorized to vary the foregoing.

No responsibility regarding messages attaches to this Company until the same are presented and accepted at one of its transmitting offices; and if a message is sent to such office by one of the Company's messengers, he acts for that purpose as the agent of the sender.

Messages will be delivered free within the established free delivery limits of the terminal office—for delivery at a greater distance, a special charge will be made to cover the cost of such delivery.

The Company will not be liable for damages in any case where the claim is not presented in writing, within sixty days after sending the message.

A. R. BREWER, Secretary.　　　　　　　　　　　　　　　　NORVIN GREEN, President.

Jan 30th 188*2*

Send the following message, subject to the above terms, which are agreed to.

To Dear Ellen.

I have only a moment before Dr Parker leaves to write you that Sallie has a bouncing boy. Poor child, she has had a very hard time. The boy was born at 8.45 P.M. and Dr. P. has been here since this A.M. Love to Sallie and her love her Mother...

☞ READ THE NOTICE AND AGREEMENT AT THE TOP.

NOTE WRITTEN ON A TELEGRAPH BLANK BY JAMES ROOSEVELT TO HIS SISTER-IN-LAW, MRS. JOHN ROOSEVELT, AND LEFT AT "ROSEDALE" BY DR. PARKER ON HIS WAY BACK TO POUGHKEEPSIE AFTER FRANKLIN'S BIRTH.

5

CHRISTENING DRESS USED AT ST. JAMES,
HYDE PARK, MARCH 20, 1882.

"We arranged the flowers beautifully and papa, mamma, and Elliott Roosevelt came up. At 11 we took darling Baby to the Chapel in his prettiest clothes and best behavior. Dr. Cady christened him 'Franklin Delano' . . . Baby was quite good and lovely, so we were proud of him."

From Sara Delano Roosevelt's diary, March 22, 1882.

6

"Baby went to his first party yesterday . . . He wanted to dance and I could hardly hold him . . . He tries to imitate Budgy and the cats, and manages to say a semblance of 'Papa' and 'Mamma'."

From Sara Delano Roosevelt's diary, November 11, 1882.

"We have a tree for everyone on the place. Franklin gave out the presents for the first time . . . We are having splendid sleighing and coasting and we do a great deal of both. Today James and I had a ride in the Portland cutter, just we two . . .James gave Baby his first coast."

From Sara Delano Roosevelt's diary, Christmas Eve, 1883.

FRANKLIN ON THE DONKEY, WITH BUDGY AND HIS NURSE MAMIE.

As a Harvard sophomore, Franklin wrote a thesis on "The Roosevelt Family in New Amsterdam," tracing the direct line back to Claes Martenszen van Roosevelt who came from Holland and settled in New Amsterdam about 1649. In 1752, Isaac Roosevelt (Claes' great-grandson) married Cornelia Hoffman of Red Hook. He lived in New York City until the Revolution, then went to Rhinebeck. With this marriage to a Red Hook girl and later

8

residence in the town of Rhinebeck, the long connection of the Roosevelt family with Dutchess County begins. Isaac was a private in the local militia, and a member of the New York convention that ratified the United States Constitution at Poughkeepsie in 1788. His portrait by Gilbert Stuart hangs over the east fireplace in the big library at Hyde Park.

Isaac's son, James, built his house in 1818 to the north of Poughkeepsie (on land now occupied by the Hudson River State Hospital). He called it "Mount Hope," and spent his summers there. His son, Isaac, F.D.R.'s grandfather and a non-practicing physician, bought "Rosedale," less than a mile north of his father's place, in 1832.

At this second Isaac's death in 1863 his younger son, John, inherited "Rosedale," and the elder son, James, F.D.R.'s father, inherited "Mount Hope." Three years later "Mount Hope" burned, and James sold the land to the State and bought "Springwood." He took his "Mount Hope" brownstone gate posts with him. You see them in this picture. The two brothers, James

MRS. ROOSEVELT GOES CALLING. SHE WAVES GOOD-
BYE TO HER HUSBAND AND TWO-YEAR-OLD FRANKLIN.

9

and John, and their families, saw much of one another, since "Springwood" was less than two miles north of "Rosedale," an easy ride on the state road or a pleasant river excursion.

*　　*　　*

Traveling was so difficult that Franklin's parents left him at home when Mr. Roosevelt had to go on business to Mexico. Franklin spent his fourth summer with his grandparents, the Warren Delanos, at "Algonac," near New-burgh. They lived in a buff and brown towered Victorian house about twenty miles south of Hyde Park on the "wrong" (west) side of the Hudson. Theirs was patriarchal family life on a scale Franklin was not used to at Hyde Park. Not only was the house larger than his own, but there were many more relatives about. His grandparents had had eleven children. Six were living at the time of this visit. His five aunts and uncles and five of his first cousins were either visiting the senior Warren Delanos, or, like the Hitches, were

10

living with them. Here we see some of the family playing the then fashionable game of croquet on the back lawn, while Mr. and Mrs. Warren Delano sit under the trees and watch the game with Franklin and other members of the younger generation playing around them. The church towers of the city of Newburgh show in the middle distance.

In the autumn, when his parents returned from their Mexican trip, Franklin's Aunt Dora (Forbes) took him to the Newburgh ferry to meet them. He was so happy to see his mother that on the way back to "Algonac" he climbed on the seat of the big wagon beside her and stood there silent all the way to his grandfather's house, his arms tight around her neck, his face close to hers. The next day the James Roosevelts drove home to Hyde Park.

FRANKLIN'S HOBBY HORSE, CALLED "MEXICO" IN HONOR OF HIS PARENTS' TRIP; MOST ANCIENT OF TOYS; A TOY THAT IS PART WORK OF ART, PART ECHO OF HISTORY; AND A FINE EXAMPLE OF AMERICANA.

THE CLIPPER SHIP "SURPRISE" ON WHICH SARA DELANO
WENT FROM NEW YORK TO HONGKONG IN 1862. FROM A
PAINTING HANGING IN F.D.R.'S STUDY

"My grandfather, who owned a fleet of rugged sailing vessels, became his own best sea captain, and my father, like his father before him, had a great affection for the sea . . .

"Then Father, (being in business in China), finding it possible to send for us, arranged that Mother, her little brood of children, and a cousin who was helping her teach us, should set sail on an old-fashioned, square-rigged clipper ship *The Surprise*, to join him in the Orient. I was naturally completely thrilled at the dramatic change in my orderly little life. To go to China! Even today, I suppose a child of eight would be thrilled at the prospect, but to us in those days, it was incredibly exciting . . .

"The *Surprise* was a fine, sturdy ship, and one that had made the voyage many times. It took us four months to round the Horn and reach China, and ours was an uneventful and easy voyage. Our lives were regulated

12

just as they had been at home. We had our lessons, our sewing, our games, our reading aloud and talks with our mother, our meals, and our early bed. There was a cow on board and chickens, and while the food was simple, it was wholesome and homelike."

From "My Boy Franklin"

This early voyage was the first of many. The James Roosevelts were a mobile family. Almost every year they would go abroad, usually on the *Celtic* or the *Germanic* for a few months — for the season in London, for the cure in Bad Neuheim, or, later, to visit Mrs. Roosevelt's sister, Mrs. Paul Forbes, in Paris. The picture shows a fraction of the ample Victorian luggage that accompanied every well-to-do family, here with its numbers "J.R. No. 1, No. 2, No. 3," and on up to the numbers required to contain properly the elaborate clothes of the period.

"I shall feel fearfully lonely when you are abroad but I shall expect to hear from you at least twice a week and shall write you on Sundays and Thursdays as usual."

From a letter by F.D.R. to his parents,
Groton, April 13, 1897.

Up the state road almost to Hyde Park village, or by the river road that passed the pond, it was just more than a mile from James Roosevelt's to Colonel Archibald Rogers' door. Here, with the grown-up family friendships, with the Rogers house filled with children, and with only six months difference in age between Edmund and Franklin, it was natural that they were always playing together. The letters, diaries and family albums record the families' and boys' intimacy. The Rogers' family life was more like that at "Algonac." There were four surviving boys and two girls, a huge pile of a house, and lots of servants, a top floor, its whole space devoted to a play hall surrounded by boys' rooms. There were many acres of woods, farms, a fine pond, and a wide expanse of river shore. With these assets, plus Mr. and Mrs. Rogers' and the children's sociability, "Crumwold" became a center for the neighboring families, the Newbolds, the Hoyts, and the Roosevelts. Their children played there, sometimes had their lessons there. They went on riding expeditions with the Colonel or the Rogers' tutor, they came there for dancing school. On these exciting winter afternoons the floor was cleared of furniture, the stuffed mountain goats and wildcats were pushed against the walls of the huge entrance hall, and the rugs were rolled up. Then the deer heads and great bear skins looked down from the dark, paneled walls, while the mothers, nurses, and governesses looked on, from the chairs along the walls, at the children's efforts to learn to dance. The neighboring children came by sleigh and even by train to this still well remembered function.

The Rogers' house parties were large, with all ages mixed. The golf course, the tennis court, the pond for skating in winter, and for swimming in summer, the boathouse on the river used for housing the *Jack Frost* and other less celebrated ice boats, the stables filled with horses — all these facilities made for a wonderfully healthy outdoor life.

WHEN FRANKLIN'S GODFATHER, CAPTAIN ELLIOTT ROOSEVELT, BROUGHT HIS LITTLE DAUGHTER ELEANOR, WHO BECAME FRANKLIN'S WIFE, TO VISIT THE JAMES ROOSEVELTS AT "SPRINGWOOD," FRANKLIN TOOK HIS TURN AT BEING THE HORSE AND CARRIED HER PIGGY BACK AROUND THE PLAYROOM.

The Hudson River has a large share in this story. It makes a structural, if fluid, backbone for our landscape. It gives individuality to our community, not only pictorially but spiritually. Up here, where it flows in front of the Catskills' elegant mass, it touches all our lives with its majestic beauty. Its presence makes our landscape unique, tremendous in scale yet intimate and livable. The River is very civilized, tactfully and sometimes craftily hiding its strength. It has carried endless traffic, from Indian canoes, to the first white man's *Half Moon*; from Hyde Park's West Indies trading-packets to Kingston's

16

whalers; from the first steamboat, the *Clermont*, to the later day and night boats to Albany. The River carried much of the valley's food into the city. When the opening of the Erie Canal enlarged the city's bread basket, the River bore, on its still frequently seen tugs and barges, produce from more distant places. It is the source of our spring industry of shad fishing, and in the Eighteen-seventies it supplied Hyde Park with its caviar industry and the sturgeon meat then known as "Albany beef." When it froze over in winter, it became a bridge between communities.

Now the river is used less, both for business and pleasure, than it used to be. During Franklin Roosevelt's youth, his family, as well as all the other families who lived along the Hudson, used it a great deal. We see James Roosevelt sailing down the river with his wife and son to visit his brother John at Rosedale." There is also a picture of the family schooner *Half Moon*. This was the first boat in a long line of boats — including a later *Half Moon* (the two were frequently mentioned in F.D.R.'s letters), small-boy ships made of nut shells, crows' nests in trees, adolescents' rafts, sailing models, college shells, canoes, warships, models for his children, pictures, prints, books about ships. Ships surely moved his consciousness when he, as a baby, first saw them on the Hudson from the windows of his home. As a little boy, too, he knew ocean liners on which he was taken to Europe. The Delanos had used ships for generations. Thus, familiarity and affection for them came quite naturally to Franklin Roosevelt.

Here we see Mrs. Roosevelt cutting off Franklin's curls. He disliked long hair — as any proper small boy should — as he also disliked velvet Lord Fauntleroy suits and kilts. He preferred sailor suits and short hair.

All the big country places had their donkey, pony or goat carts for the little children. This one is a "hand-me-down" from half-brother "Rosy" (James Roosevelt Roosevelt, twenty-eight years Franklin's senior and just the age of Franklin's mother). The picture shows the old "Springwood" house as you saw it from the front. When the house was remodeled in 1914 the tower gave way to the new stone wing which now contains the big library. The west side of the house, facing the river, was not greatly changed. Even today that facade shows vestiges of its former Victorian look. It still has an informal charm that is characteristic of Hudson River Bracketed. Its face wasn't lifted for twenty-six years. When Franklin was little, the clapboard siding was painted a tasteful Downing buff with shutters and trim a rich chocolate — the ground floor rooms were shaded by comfortable vine covered verandahs. The arched window with the balcony was the east exposure of Franklin's large play and school room on the top floor of the tower. It was known as the Tower Room. The room directly below was his mother's bedroom.

FRANKLIN AND HIS FATHER SNOWSHOEING TO THE ROGERS'
AFTER THE BLIZZARD OF 1888.

"James took Franklin out ice-boating . . . James coasted with Franklin yesterday and the day before. F and I snow-shoed to the Rogers', snow a foot deep, such a snow has fallen that F built a tunnel, working nearly all day at it . . . Poor little Mlle. Sandoz had such an upset tobogganing that she came home sad and quite black and blue. Franklin seemed to think it quite a joke."

From Sara Delano Roosevelt's diary, March 18, 1888.

"My dear Mamma:

"We are going to fish this afternoon, this morning I take the goat cart, to give, mary newbold, a drive, we miss you very much. Your affectionate son
"Franklin"

*From letter by F.D.R. to Sara
Delano Roosevelt, Spring, 1888.*

Sometimes the family would row down the river, in the afternoon, to visit the John Roosevelts at "Rosedale." It was almost a mile of hot, wood walk to the house near the Post Road. This house is now much as it was in F.D.R.'s youth, when the families would have tea there and big cousin Ellie would supervise Franklin. The Post Road (or the State Road, as it was called and should be called now) was a very different one in those days. It started, as you remember, as an Indian trail from New Amsterdam to Fort Orange.

Over this same trail, in 1703, the provincial legislature authorized the construction of a "Publick and Common General Highway to extend from King's Bridge in the County of Westchester through the same County of Westchester, Dutchess County and the County of Albany of the breadth of four rods . . ." By a special dispensation, until 1713 Dutchess County, being so sparsely settled, had only to maintain a highway wide enough for horse and man. On this track, in the Seventeen-forties, the post rider made his weekly trip from New York to Albany. In the Eighteenth-century most of the settlements were very near the Post Road. Even in James Roosevelt's day the traffic was not too disturbing. I remember the highway as a narrow, curvy, dirt road, which during my lifetime has straightened itself out, has broadened and armored its surface, and has become Route 9, a great artery of heavy traffic.

THE JAMES ROOSEVELTS ARE WALKING UP THE PATH FROM THE "ROSEDALE" BOATHOUSE WHILE FRANKLIN CUTS ACROSS THE LAWN.

In this picture the James Roosevelts are coasting with Taddy and Helen on the hill back of the gardener's cottage. (Taddy and Helen were Franklin's nephew and niece, children of his half-brother, "Rosy"; they were also, respectively, three years and one year older than their uncle.) From the top of the hill, under proper conditions, one would sometimes slide to the river, slide through the primeval forest almost to the railroad siding where many years later, as President, Franklin was to greet prime ministers and refugee royalty. He enjoyed especially driving them up through his beloved forest, for it is one of the few stands in this part of the county which has never been timbered off. It looks now as it must have looked on September 28, 1609, when Henry Hudson sailed up the hitherto undiscovered river that was to bear his name, and anchored his *Half Moon* off Crum Elbow Point.

*   *   *

Franklin's treasure-chest was given to him by his grand-father. In it he kept a great-uncle's 1812 sailor's hat, a brass cannon, a model of the *Constitution*, and the small figurehead of a ship, which he is showing off to Helen and Taddy in the Tower room. The lid of every child's box, even though the contents be well worn and familiar, hides a mystery. A boy's real sea chest, like this one, holds even more than the magic of Pandora's box. It is part of a ship; it is filled with sea winds and treasured relics of history. No matter how familiar, they become strange and exciting for being hidden and covered up; the treasure is a treasure, the boy a collector.

Franklin and Edmund Rogers playing hide-and-seek in the primeval forest, near the brook where frogs and minnows were sometimes caught, where the water was unusually clear, in which some unexpected crawfish or shell might turn up, where ferns and jack-in-the-pulpit uncurled in Spring, where it was always cool and mysterious. The memory of the woods in which we played as children freshens our spirits later.

Sebastian Bowman, Roosevelt gardener for about 30 years (retired in 1897) tending the roses in the old greenhouse — roses whose descendants are still in the "new" greenhouse! They adorn the same blue bowl we saw Miss Sara Delano arranging on her first visit to "Springwood." It is fitting that they, too, should have continuity. The roses of the Dutch coat-of-arms, the seed of their seed, on the dining-room table for tourists to admire.

Franklin in the crow's nest and Edmund on the ground firing a wooden cannon; they are playing naval battles.

"The tree where F.D.R. and I rigged up our ship," writes Edmund Rogers, "was a hemlock close to the driveway and just outside the garden where he is buried."

"Franklin had a great habit of ordering his playmates around and for reasons which I have never been able to fathom, was generally permitted to have his way. I know that I, overhearing him one day with a little boy on the place, with whom he was digging a fort, said to him:

" 'My son, don't give the orders all the time, let the other boys give them sometime.'

" 'Mummie,' he said to me without guile, lifting a soiled, streaked face, 'if I don't give the orders, nothing will happen!' "

From "My Boy Franklin".

DRAWING OF A SAILBOAT (ONE OF MANY PICTURES OF BOATS) MADE BY FRANKLIN WHEN HE WAS SEVEN; IT WAS ENCLOSED IN A LETTER TO HIS MOTHER.

29

Before breakfast on his seventh birthday, Franklin finds his new pony, Debby, in the stable. He had to promise to take care of her, as he had had to do with Marksman, his red setter puppy. If such stables exist at all now, they are a sporting luxury. Then they housed the families' only means of transportation, for both business and pleasure. This applied to the one-horse farm as well as to the great river estate. A child who has not sat behind a dashboard, held the reins and red-lashed whip and watched the rhythmical motion of a horse's rump, with the harness etched by white foam, who has not been surrounded by the horse's smell on a hot August afternoon, or been thrilled by the sleighbells and the runners' smooth crunch after the winter's first snowstorm, has missed one of life's experiences. The studio I use now was my grandfather's red clapboard stable in which his three horses were kept; one for the buckboard, two to ride. In my childhood, my parents' much grander stable was an integral part of our life. Though motors started to supplant carriages when I was a small boy, all the big places still had elaborate stables, stables very like the one in this picture. I remember the delicious, leathery smell of the yellow-varnished-wood harness rooms, with their brackets for saddles and bridles, and their wall cases, backed with green felt, for the polished set pieces of sleigh bells and dyed plumes. There were huge coach houses with numbers of elegant and graceful Brewster vehicles — a basket phaeton with white-fringed top, a buckboard, smart green buggies with red or yellow wheels, and a number of sleighs. Some of these conveyances are now on display in the basement at the Franklin D. Roosevelt Library. One of the grooms would be charged with the duty of making a stencil picture, in colored sands, on the cement floor in front of the vehicles. This sand stencil would be destroyed every time a vehicle was used.

Then, of course, there were the horses in their select box or more numerous open stalls, with a fine, white-fenced paddock outside. When the horses went out with the family, their manes and tails were beautifully brushed, their hoofs were varnished, and often their ankles were wrapped in white puttees. You could see your reflection in their harness with the silver crests polished as if for Saturday inspection. When they returned from the drive, two or more grooms would clean the horses and curry them, with much whistling and puffing, a sort of professional song — or, rather, noise — of which the grooms were inordinately proud, and which, incidentally, gave the impression that they were working very hard. When motors started to supplant carriages, coachmen became very reluctant chauffeurs.

*   *   *

Composition by young Franklin: "The horse, which is a donkey sometimes, but as a rule is a noble animal. A horse has to be fed on hay, oats, bran and grass. If I bought a horse, I would put him in the stable and have him groomed and washed every day as a well groomed horse is always more healthy than a dirty horse but I would be careful not to let any soap get in his eyes because he would scream if I did."

FRANKLIN HAS JUST COME BACK FROM A RIDE
THROUGH THE WOODS ON HIS PONY DEBBY.

One day, when out riding, Franklin heard Colonel Archibald Rogers' hunt go by. He evidently did not know or remember that his father was riding with the hounds that morning. Though uninvited, he followed the grown ups on their horses just as fast as he could make his pony gallop, and at the end brought Debby in all of a lather. Mr. Roosevelt peremptorily ordered him home. Franklin had to give Debby the very best of care, for in this ill advised adventure she had caught a bad chill. Fortunately, after a week of careful nursing Debby recovered, much to the little boy's joy and relief.

*   *   *

"I dread going home to find no more Debby in her stall but I suppose it is for the best."

From a letter by F.D.R. to Sara Delano
Roosevelt, Groton, February 11, 1900.

Little Franklin found the rear seat very chilly in spite of the sleigh's historic background. It was given by Alexander II of Russia to Napoleon III and used by him and the Empress Eugénie for rides in the Bois de Boulogne. James Roosevelt bought it after the Commune in 1872, paying $15 for it at a Paris auction. It is now on exhibition in the Library.

"When he was about ten, Mrs. Roosevelt . . . found him propped up in bed, on his knees the heavy dictionary that usually stood on a stand in the library.

" 'What on earth!' she asked, 'are you doing with the dictionary up here?'

" 'Reading it,' the boy replied, 'There are lots of words that I don't understand, so I thought I would find out what they meant. I'm almost half way through'."

From "Gracious Lady," by Rita Halle Kleeman.

34

Early books: *The Book of Common Prayer* inscribed to Franklin D. Roosevelt from his mother, in 1890; *The Kindergarten Children* from Uncle Fred and Aunt Annie, Christmas, 1885; *The World of Romance* (1892) from Mrs. Edwardes, London, July, 1895; *Birds of Eastern North America*, by Frank Chapman, Christmas, 1895, and, I suspect, later and more surreptitious reading — *Beadle's Half Dime Library; Five-Point Phil; The Pavement Prince*, and similar thrillers. The large books is, of course, Noah Webster's Dictionary of 1887, which he was reading in bed.

The children's books in the picture are interesting quite apart from their contents, as one of many examples of Mrs. James Roosevelt's mania for accumulation. Historians should be grateful to her and to her son. He inherited and also expanded her collector's instincts. The mass of family photographs, documents, or mementos is simply formidable. It is fortunate that this is so. But not many families would have kept all these objects. It is safe to say that no other President of the United States ever hung in his bedroom the mounted tail of one of his father's trotting horses. This was, of course, the celebrated Gloster, which was the first to trot a mile in less than two-twenty, and was sold later to Senator Leland Stanford, of California.

"My pony Debby is well and I rode 12 miles today with papa and we are going to ride to Algonac as we did last summer," wrote F.D.R. to his mother on April 10, 1891. Franklin and his father would ride down from Hyde Park to "Algonac," to lunch and spend the day with the boy's grandparents. As you will remember, "Algonac" is just north of Newburgh and a good twenty miles away, with a ferry trip thrown in.

*   *   *

"His father never laughed at him. With him — yes, often. They were such a gay pair when they went off on long rides together. But Franklin's tragedies became his father's woes, and I've often marvelled at his success in stifling a very natural merriment over some of our son's minor disasters . . . it was the highest ideal I could hold up before our boy, to grow to be like his father, straight and honorable, just and kind, an upstanding American."

From "My Boy Franklin".

"I remember father telling the story of himself as a little boy (my guess is around ten) when one winter he was coming home on his pony via the Rogers' pond. He had spent the day visiting Edmund Rogers. Snow had fallen all day, and it was getting dark when he started home. He had not realized how much snow had fallen during that time. He and the pony got caught time and again in the drifts. Father used to describe how his pony's belly was buried in the snow, how he got off, got in front of the pony and tugged and tugged on the reins while the pony lunged forward and then fell in again. He, of course, finally got out, but it must have been quite an experience, as he used to tell the story up until the very end."

From a letter by Mrs. John
Boettiger, daughter of F.D.R.

37

Here is a picture of the Roosevelt houses as they looked before Franklin was born and until the house on the left, "Springwood," was remodelled in 1914. The "Rosy" Roosevelts', or "Red House," as it is called, appears on the right. It has changed very little over the years. The high land on which both houses were built, rolls down easily to the primeval forest. The upset bobsled on the hill illustrates the incident described in Franklin's first journalistic effort, a typewritten sheet which he christened *The Hyde Park Herald*, of January 1, 1891.

"The *Graphic* has arrived this morning.

"It snowed this morning.

"The thermometer is 14 degrees. Probae (sic) it will freeze tomorrow. Good coasting at Hyde Park on the Hudson, N. Y.—Jas. Roosevelt upset a large bob with 6 ladies and 1 boy. The boy scraped his leg a little but it is not a very bad wound. Mrs. Jas. Roosevelt and Miss Anna Roosevelt both hurt their hips. They probably will be well in two weeks . . .

"Hard rain tomorrow.

"Mr. and Mrs. J. Roosevelt will probably not go to New York tomorrow.

"Not much snow melted . . . Hard rain in New York day before yesterday. A boy was kicked in the head by a horse while he was coasting."

It was the custom, until fairly recently, for the children of the River families to be taught at home, certainly in the summer and sometimes, as in the case of Franklin Roosevelt, all year round. Here, he is a ten-year-old boy having lessons in the Tower room from Mlle. Sandoz, his Swiss governess. He had several governesses and tutors before he finally entered Groton's third form when he was fourteen.

* * *

Hyde Park, Feb. 27th, 1892

"My Darling mumkin and Pap!

"Good morning I hope you have used Pear's Soap & are flourishing now. I am dying of school fever and you will be horrified to hear that my temperature is 150.° But really I have got a 'Petit rhume' only I am in the hands of the celebrated Dr. Sandoz.— He came up to see me this morning and

ordered 5 drops of camfer on sugar twice in the mornin; a hot toe bag, breakfast in bed & stay home all day tomorrow and today if not clear of the disease. I went to play with E. yesterday and rided over there. — Today the whole army of carpenters come to lunch. — We got 12 eggs yesterday and there is no clocking hen. I can't write any more, So Good bye. Your affectionate
                                        Roosevelt Delano Franklin
P.S. The thermometer went down to 10° last night. High wind all night."
Letter from F.D.R. to his parents.

"Do not concern yourselves in the least, I won't let Franklin go out and will take good care of him; he is as gay as a finch and actually he is hardly sick at all.— He changed his clothes yesterday when he came in and I couldn't see that he had a cold but he said he had one. — I was a little distrustful because yesterday he had told me laughingly that he would be ill and wouldn't be able to go to church . . ."
Note by Mlle. Sandoz, in French, on reverse of letter.

Hyde Park, February 21, 1893
"Dear Mademoiselle:
    "What sort of a trip did you have? Was the sea rough? How many and what sort of people did you have in your cabin? And how much did the trip cost? Were you seasick? . . . I hope you found your friends well in Switzerland. Miss Inkstand is not at all nice. She comes from China . . . I would very much like to know who is the President of Switzerland? Is there a representative of each canton in the Federal Assembly? How many counsellors are there in the Federal Assembly and how many Senators for each Canton? I have to go out now. Hoping that you will reply to all my questions,
                        I am your faithful
                                Tlevesoor
                        (Roosevelt spelt backwards)
    Letter in French from F.D.R. to Mlle. Sandoz.

Ice cutting was a yearly performance on all country places, and there was, as well, the large-scale cutting that went on in the River. This river ice was stored in huge gray and yellow warehouses. The activity was picturesque — high hip boots, huge saws, and ice cakes floating in canals of black water, and poked with spears; cakes hooked to pulleys and hauled up into the houses. The private ice cutting on ponds and creeks was the same, only on

42

a smaller scale. Here we see a cake sliding on a ramp to its place in the sleigh to be taken to the hay and sawdust-filled ice house. Both the Roosevelts and the Rogers had ice houses up the hill. In summer the cool air and peculiar woody smell were always mysterious. Franklin must have remembered with pleasure John Irving (the head farmer to whom he is talking), for a photograph of him and his team hangs in F.D.R.'s bedroom.

It's lunch time, and Franklin's Uncle John with his daughter, Ellen, and his guests, Messrs. Edwards and Sanford and Dr. Burren, have come from ice boating to the little tenant cottage almost on the railroad tracks, where Mr. Roosevelt kept a room for his picnic lunches. This is a good example of the importance given to their sport by the River families in the Eighteen-nineties. John Roosevelt wanted to eat near the river, and quickly, in order to take advantage of a favorable wind. Through the window you can see Franklin on his way in to join the lunch party. Behind him is the old boathouse, and on the river is the *Icicle*, with other ice boats waiting to go out again. He also sailed from this boathouse often in other seasons.

43

"One evening Franklin was lying on the floor of his mother's writing room sorting and pasting a package of stamps that had come from Uncle Frank in Egypt. For a long time he had been waiting for some of those stamps. His brows were knit. He would turn a page in his album, go through the package examining the stamps and then turn back to the album.

"His mother, who was reading a story about the Pharaohs, let her voice dwindle away into silence. Franklin looked up inquiringly.

" 'I stopped' she said, 'because I don't believe you are hearing a word I am reading.'

"There was a wicked glint in Franklin's eyes.

"He recited with all the hard words the last two sentences his mother had read.

" 'That's really wonderful, son,' she said, 'How ever can you do that and work so intently on your stamps at the same time?'

" 'Why, I'd be ashamed', replied Franklin, 'if I couldn't do at least two things at once'."

From "Young Franklin Roosevelt," by Rita Halle Kleeman.

*   *   *

"He always had a happy faculty for saying the right thing and, at the age of four, although later he took a more modest view, he was not averse to letting you know he thought so."

From "My Boy Franklin".

*   *   *

Stamp collecting was one of F.D.R.'s most important hobbies. During the long administration of this philatelist, the government gained a considerable income from new stamp issues. His mother had started a stamp collection, when, a little girl of five, she was taken by her father to China. Later her younger brother Frederick got it. He in turn gave what had become a fairly good collection to nephew Franklin when the latter, at nine, showed real interest. While he was President he valued his collection at "perhaps $15,000." It was appraised after his death at $80,000, and sold at auction for over $230,000.

There are a great many birds around Hyde Park. Perhaps not more than other places, but surely many local citizens are unusually bird-conscious; they feed the birds in winter and build houses for their nesting in spring. There have always been amateur ornithologists about. I even remember mass meetings of the Rhinebeck Bird Club. It is more than high time to conserve and protect our birds, for some, like the wild pigeon which in the Eighteenth-century used literally to darken the sun by the density of its flights, are rarely seen now. James Roosevelt took a lively interest in all forms of nature and outdoor life. His example undoubtedly influenced his son. In addition, Franklin had a personal and active urge to know about birds. When he was eleven, he asked his father for a gun and with it shot one specimen only of each local bird. Before he was fourteen he had made a collection of three hundred Dutchess County birds. (He even sent a few to the American Museum

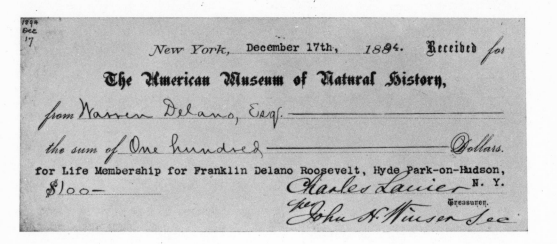

New York, December 17th, 1894. Received for

The American Museum of Natural History,

from Warren Delano, Esq. ————————————————

the sum of One hundred ———————————————— Dollars.

for Life Membership for Franklin Delano Roosevelt, Hyde Park-on-Hudson, N. Y.

$100—

Charles Lanier
Treasurer.
per John H. Winser Sec

of Natural History) .You can see this collection in a large wall case in the front hall at Hyde Park. Hovering over the case is the sparrow hawk I've drawn (mentioned several times in his letters from Groton), and inside the case you'll find a pair of small screech owls. He learned to stuff the specimens. He also kept a diary in which he noted the birds he'd seen each day. His grandfather, Warren Delano, gave him a life membership in the Natural History Society as a reward for his enthusiastic, efficient, and thorough handling of this hobby.

"Such was his interest in his hobby that he determined to learn how to stuff and preserve the specimens himself. I do not believe he quite knew what he was letting himself in for . . . but once having decided he would learn to mount birds, nothing would induce him to give up the notion.

"I could tell in many ways that in his heart he was ready to abandon the taxidermist's profession almost as soon as he was launched upon it. He had not realized when he started to learn that the process was in some ways very unpleasant, but he stuck to it, even though sometimes he turned rather green, until he was sure he could do it, and do it well. Immediately the fact was established to his satisfaction, however, the remaining specimens were mounted elsewhere."

From "My Boy Franklin".

"I hope you will seal up my birds before the babies come to stay with you or else I should be afraid of the consequences."

From letter by F.D.R. to his parents, Groton, February 25, 1897.

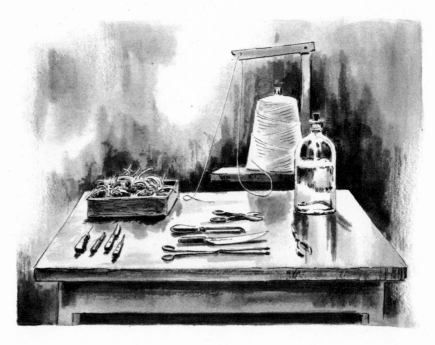

48

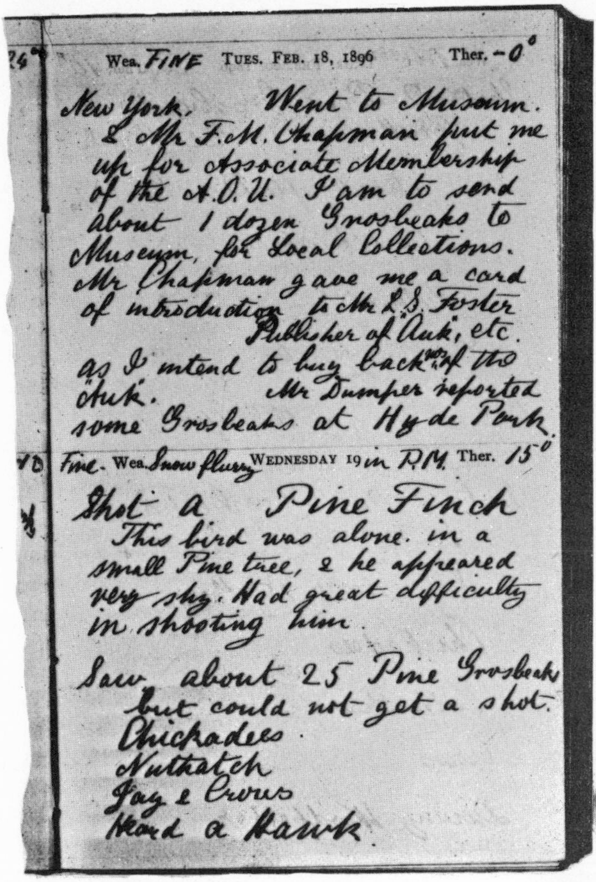

Wea. *FINE* TUES. FEB. 18, 1896 Ther. *-0°*

New York.   Went to Museum.
& Mr F.M. Chapman put me
up for Associate Membership
of the A.O.U. I am to send
about 1 dozen Grosbeaks to
Museum, for Local Collections.
Mr Chapman gave me a card
of introduction to Mr L.S. Foster
        Publisher of Auk, etc.
as I intend to buy back the
"Auk".   Mr Dumper reported
some Grosbeaks at Hyde Park

Fine. Wea. Snow flurry WEDNESDAY 19 in P.M. Ther. *15°*

Shot a   Pine Finch
  This bird was alone. in a
small Pine tree, & he appeared
very shy. Had great difficulty
in shooting him.

Saw about 25 Pine Grosbeak
  but could not get a shot.
  Chickadees.
  Nuthatch
  Jay & Crows
  Heard a Hawk

PAGE FROM FRANKLIN'S
SMALL BIRD DIARY.

TWO SCREECH OWLS
FROM THE CASE OF
STUFFED BIRDS IN THE
HALL AT "SPRINGWOOD".

49

The Roosevelts' nearest neighbors were the Thomas Newbolds. The two houses are less than a quarter of a mile apart; the Newbold house is due north. You can see it now from the State Road, and through the hedge as you drive to the Library. The house used to look as you see it in the picture, not as it does now. On the back lawn was a grass tennis court which is the subject of a picture on one of the following pages. Mary Newbold was Franklin's contemporary. She is mentioned frequently in his early letters. Her father, Thomas Jefferson Newbold, had been elected as a Democrat to the State Senate four years before Franklin was born. He was the last Dutchess County Democrat to win this seat until thirty-two years later, in 1910, when Franklin Roosevelt started his political career.

In the picture, Mary and Franklin are circling the Newbold turn-around without holding on to their handle-bars. A quarter of that bicycle ride was on the State Road. That they could ride fearlessly points up the difference in traffic between 1896 and today. Franklin got his first bicycle when he was twelve years old.

* * *

"I am going to buy a new bicycle! A Columbia chainless for $60 as I shall do a good deal of riding this summer going to the Hotel etc., and shall need a good wheel at Cambridge next year. I thought this a chance, as the wheel costs ordinarily $75."

From letter by F.D.R. to his parents, Groton, June 20, 1900.

Fourteen-year-old Franklin and Mary Newbold are canoeing on the Hudson. The River was an intimate part of the lives of those who lived near it; it was frequently used for swimming and all kinds of boating. In Mrs. James Roosevelt's diary she mentions going out in a canoe with Franklin after dinner.

51

"As I have been sitting on the platform here today, I have been thinking of the time nearly a century and a half ago when Governor Morgan Lewis, who lived here in the town of Hyde Park, was chiefly responsible for starting the Union free-school system for the children of the State of New York. This township, therefore, can claim a kind of sponsorship for free and universal school education in New York.

"My mind has gone back also to the days when I used to spend many hours as a small boy holding my father's horse in the village of Hyde Park while my father attended meetings of the school board. Long before those days, back in 1870, my father had helped, with very great pride, to build the red brick school over in the village, where it still stands, and it was considered a model in its day."

From address made by F.D.R. to a teachers' conference in the Franklin D. Roosevelt High School, Hyde Park, October 5, 1940.

This hill south of "Crumwold" is one of the finest for coasting in these parts. This picture shows it as it looked any winter between 1894 and 1904. Coasting would start at the great elm on the southwest corner of the lawn. From there to the edge of the woods, behind the spectator, was a long expanse of open hill. On big days, the farm sleigh would drag the lazy up hill, which afforded an exceptional luxury. Besides the usual means of sliding down hill, the children would sit on large tin trays or pie pans, which gave an especially intriguing corkscrew motion as they bumped and swirled to the bottom — if they were lucky enough to get all the way down. The complications of Hunt's

Victorian-Loire-Château style — with, as F.D.R. used to tell, a porch put around to squash it down — show well from this view.

"There was a period," Edmund Rogers wrote, "when four of us studied and were tutored in the 'Crumwold' school room. The four were F.D.R., Mortimer and Frederick Ashton, sons of Dr. Ashton, the rector of St. James Church, and me.

"We had a tutor, Leon D. Bonnet, who later became head of a boys' school in Tuxedo Park, N. Y. These classes lasted, I think, for a couple of years when we were about 10 to 12 years of age."

Skating is one sport that has changed very little over the years. Except for the clothes, this scene might have taken place on our "Glenburn" pond in my youth. Then there would be most exciting hockey games between arctic goal posts, where you'd have the experts, home from school or college, playing with the fathers and the children. Every kind of skating would be in evidence, from the lady with weak ankles pushing a chair on runners, to the skillful "outer-

edger." There would be games of touch-tag and snap-the-whip. All this going on at once, while on the bank you'd find a roaring fire of logs, with other logs around to sit on between games, or when you were putting on your skates. This pond of the Rogers' was particularly convenient for the neighbors, as it lay half way between "Crumwold" and the Newbold and Roosevelt houses. These families and their guests would crowd it in winter.

F.D.R.'s interest in trees was of long standing. Both his father and Colonel Rogers were tree lovers, and on both places the results of their care are obvious to the most casual visitor. On the Bard place, too (now the Frederick Vanderbilt mansion) those Eighteenth century doctors had made the first arboretum in this country. The beauty of their trees is still a joy to see. In this picture, Franklin, Edmund, and his father are cutting out a huge dead tree, preparatory to replanting. They would ride through the woods in winter with ropes tied to their saddles, and with them the horses would be tethered — as Edmund is doing here — or they would be used to help in felling a tree. As some of the "Crumwold" windows had transparent pictures of Indians, and the walls were adorned with various Western scenes, as well as with hunting trophies, I suspect that one of the reasons for these ropes had its origin in the romantic West.

Many of the larger places had each its tennis court. This one is on the lawn back of the Newbold house, and as you can see now when you are at the Roosevelt Library, it is only a step from the Roosevelts to the Newbolds. Here Franklin usually played, (as the Roosevelt court was not made until 1915), and so would his two cousins, Uncle John's girls, who were at one time the woman champions of the United States. There was often a group of spectators, and there was cutting in and out of games. There were iced tea and barley water and sandwiches in the shade under the trees. Now it seems funny to us to see people playing tennis in long skirts and dark trousers, but here in our not very dressy community they would play tennis dressed as we see them, or go sailing with neckties and high, starched collars.

It was during this period that F.D.R. was working on the *Crimson* at Harvard and "going out" intensively in Boston or New York.

In an editorial in the *Crimson* dated September 30, 1903, he wrote: "It is this idea of responsibility which every Freshman should keep constantly before him. Responsibility to the University, to his class, to himself; and the only way to fulfill this is to be always active . . . Every man should have a wholesome horror of that happy-go-lucky state of doing nothing but enough classroom work to keep off probation. It is not so much brilliance as effort that is appreciated here; determination to accomplish something."

The American Challenge Pennant for Ice-Yacht Racing was placed in competition one year before Franklin Roosevelt was born. John Roosevelt and Colonel Rogers were two of the leaders in the sport, which flourished greatly on the River for the next twenty-five years. It is still indulged in. The Hudson, North Shrewsbury, Orange Lake, Newburgh, and Carthage Ice Yacht Clubs took their sport with the greatest seriousness. The gentlemen who belonged to these clubs spent much time and money improving their boats, and frequently building new ones. So there are whole families of *Jack Frosts*, *Icicles* or *Avalanches*. Jacob E. Buckhout, of Poughkeepsie, was the most famous of the builders, and is also frequently mentioned among the racers.

The New York Times found this sport worth reporting at length. For example, on March 20, 1885, we read: "The speed of the yachts reached more than a mile a minute . . . the event of the day was the wrecking of Archie Rogers' *Jack Frost*, one of the fastest boats in the country . . ." Or, again, "Mr. Buckhout's *Willie* made fearful speed down the river this noon, beating a passenger train from here to New Hamburg . . ." When, in 1903, Mr. and Mrs. Rogers had a close shave, the story was printed in great detail. The following quotation from Henry A. Buck's article in the *Badminton Library* amusingly suggests the excitement there was about iceboat racing:

"Suddenly, an express train is seen dashing its way along the banks of the opposite shore. At once the helm is turned, and the vessel bounds forward eager for the race. In a moment or two the yacht is alongside the train, the engineer salutes and pulls the trottle of his iron steed wide open, the passengers wave their handkerchiefs, the challenge is accepted, the helmsman puts the yacht about, and the race is begun. The wind along the shore is puffy and changeable, and for a moment the train seems to be leaving us behind; but, as we round a bend in the river the full force of the wind is felt once more, and the yacht dashes ahead of the train, now teeming with excited passengers, as if the engineer were running at half-speed instead of at his greatest. Still another moment and the train is hidden from view by an intervening cliff and tunnel, and when the smoke of the engine is observed again, the ice-yacht is too far ahead to give even the semblance of a contest to what promised to be an exciting and close race. The yacht is eased and drops back again alongside the train, the engineer salutes his conqueror with three shrill whistles, and another race is begun, only to end as before."

In the announcements of ice yachts and their owners from 1902 on, you will find Franklin Roosevelt's name with that of his boat, the lateen-rigged *Hawk* (built by Buckhout), in which we see him racing the Rogers' *Jack Frost*. This was, of course, an uneven race; for the boats were quite obviously in different classes, the *Jack Frost* being one of the largest of the ice yachts and the *Hawk* a small one. You can see the *Hawk* now in the Roosevelt Library.

"Franklin used to take turns playing Santa Claus with my brothers. This year, 1901, was his turn. The week before Christmas found two little girls sneaking up to the forbidden third floor. Poking among the open trunks filled with tinsel and glistening balls would do no harm. But what was in this trunk — this red stuff and all the funny white hair? So there was no Santa Claus! The little girls crept downstairs, an empty feeling in their hearts.

"A week later, on Christmas Eve, Ann (Rogers) and Helen (Huntington) went upstairs to the third floor to the glittering Christmas tree with its hundreds of candles and its shining ornaments; its French dolls, monkeys on sticks, and all of Schwarz's famous toys peeping out from every branch. Then came the hush, the jingle bells, the cheers as that jovial Santa Claus burst in swinging his pack to the floor and handing out the big red balls, trumpets, drums, dolls and bags of marbles. As he was leaving, Ann was told to kiss Santa good-bye. Ann held back but eventually, being a good little girl, she went reluctantly up to him and kissed — not a smooth cheek but a rough mask!

"No doubts left now: Helen and Ann could be seen together, talking earnestly 'all my brothers are in the room — it must be Franklin'— and so it was."

From "Christmas Tree in the 'Crumwold' Playroom," an account written for the Franklin D. Roosevelt Library, by Mrs. Griswold Webb (the youngest of the Rogers family).

This rustic pavilion on the Rogers' pond — we have seen it twice already — always fascinated me. It was the perfect background for the well and completely dressed bather. Against it the ladies with their long black stockings and frilled bathing suits looked just right. It's a wonderful pond to swim in, and while I was drawing around "Crumwold" I would go in in the middle of the day. In this picture you have Edmund Rogers, his father, and F.D.R. chatting in the shade, Mary Newbold and her little sister coming into the summer house, while Ellen Roosevelt suns herself on the dock and "Rosy" Roosevelt swims.

The house on the opposite page is the Hall place above Tivoli, New York, where Anna Eleanor Roosevelt was brought up by her grandmother and her aunts. Although Eleanor and Franklin had known each other as little children, it was at a dance in 1898 at the Orange (New Jersey) Country Club, that they met again, after they had not seen each other for several years. At about this time, when there was to be a house party at Hyde Park, Franklin wrote to his parents from Groton, saying:

"How about Teddy Robinson and Eleanor Roosevelt? They would go well and help to fill out chinks."

"We loved the house and place at Tivoli. When my aunts and uncles were at home, life was pleasant indeed. I did have to run errands for them, and many times a day I ran along the little path that went through the woods to our stable."

From "This is My Story," by Eleanor Roosevelt.

* * *

8 East 76th Street, N. Y., Dec. 2, 1903, Wednesday.
"Dearest Cousin Sally,

"I must write you and thank you for being so good to me yesterday. I know just how you feel and how hard it must be, but I do so want you to learn to love me a little. You must know that I will always try to do what you wish for I have grown to love you very dearly during the past summer.

"It is impossible for me to tell you how I feel toward Franklin, I can only say that my one great wish is always to prove worthy of him.

"I am counting the days to the 12th when I hope Franklin & you will both be here again & if there is anything which I can do for you you will write me, won't you?

"With much love, dear Cousin Sally,
Always devotedly,
ELEANOR"
Letter from Eleanor Roosevelt to her future mother-in-law.

63

Friday.

"Dearest Mama —

". . . I know what pain I must have caused you and you know I wouldn't do it if I really could have helped it . . . That's all that could be said — I know my mind, have known it for a long time, and know that I could never think otherwise: Result: I am the happiest man just now in the world; likewise the luckiest.—And for you, dear Mummy, you know that nothing can ever change what we have always been & always will be to each other — only now you have two children to love & to love you — and Eleanor as you know will always be a daughter to you in every true way . . .

Your ever loving

F.D.R."

From letter to his mother, dated Harvard "Crimson," December 4, 1903.

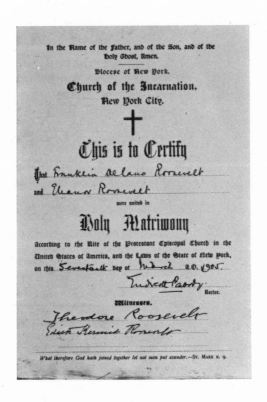

64

As a young married couple, the Franklin Roosevelts lived in New York at the Hotel Webster, while F.D.R. attended the Columbia Law School. They moved into Mrs. James Roosevelt's house when she went to Hyde Park in the early spring, and spent most of their week-ends at Hyde Park with her. After their delayed honeymoon in Europe, they settled at 25 East 36th Street, in a house bought and prepared for them by Mrs. Roosevelt. Anna and James were born there. F.D.R. entered Carter, Ledyard and Milburn's office in 1907 after he'd been admitted to the bar. First he was managing clerk, later he specialized in admiralty law. One summer the young Roosevelts rented a house at Seabright, New Jersey, but although they enjoyed the sea-bathing, they found they preferred Hyde Park. F.D.R. helped his mother run the farm. He wanted to do this as a business, but she insisted it be run as a gentleman's estate. Consequently, he bought up pieces of land adjoining the property, and about 1910 started his experiments in forestry. He joined the Hyde Park Volunteer Fire Brigade, and discussed politics in the Dutchess County Society.

The Franklin Roosevelts went to the neighbors' parties as he had always done. The Rogers' New Year's Eve party was a local institution. As a child, I remember mother and father, all dressed up in evening dress, going to it. When my sister and I came down on the morning of the New Year to see them, they would give us noisy paper trumpets, rattles and caps, loot from the night's celebration.

*　　*　　*

From Hyde Park village you go north on the State Road for about half a mile to St. James Church. It was built in 1846 from plans made by Augustus Cowman, one of those extraordinarily versatile Hyde Park characters, who was also the publisher of a Poughkeepsie newspaper. He went abroad for two years to study church architecture in England, and upon his return not only designed the building and supervised its construction, but materially assisted in the financing of St. James. In this simple country church, he created one of the charming ecclesiastical buildings of the period.

St. James was an integral part of Franklin Roosevelt's life. Its setting, the sense of age and tradition inside and out, make it an unusually distinguished symbol of its denomination. In our county, the Dutch Reformed and Lutheran churches usually have age and style. The Episcopalian buildings are relatively new and pretentious imitations of Tudor country churches. But St. James has a dignity and restraint of which the edifices of the late gilded age are incapable. It bears the marks of its more than a century's service to the community.

On the south corner of the church's land hangs the familiar ecclesiastical black sign. Some years ago, over the gilt lettering, "Church of the President," a wag chalked, "formerly God's." F.D.R. told this story on himself with great gusto.

Inside, St. James has as satisfying a style as it has outside. Its traditions are underlined by the memorial plaques to the Bards and the Tellers, the Hoyts and the Rogers, and many other local families. Even if they have

ST. JAMES CHURCH FROM THE STATE ROAD.

INTERIOR OF ST. JAMES CHURCH.

68

not lived all their lives in our community, most of them have returned to be buried here. The large plaque to the left of the chancel is a memorial of General Morgan Lewis, Governor of New York, whose monument is outside. He and Samuel Bard (the distinguished physician whose house was just north of the church) were its first wardens. Later, James Roosevelt was both vestryman and warden, and certainly F.D.R. followed in the tradition when he became vestryman in 1906 and succeeded Archibald Rogers as senior warden in 1928. The little vestry room, opening from the left side of the chancel, with its old records, documents and dated ecclesiastical furniture, smells deliciously of age and history.

When you go into the church, you see President Roosevelt's memorial plaque to the right of the chancel. The Roosevelt pew is third from the front on the left side.

*   *   *

"I do remember once, when the children were still very young, asking him solemnly how much religion he felt we should teach them, or whether it was our duty to leave them free minds until they decided for themselves as they grew older. He looked at me with his amused and quizzical smile, and said that he thought they had better go to church and learn what he had learned. It would do them no harm. I replied, 'But are you sure that you believe in everything you learned?' He answered, 'I really never thought about it. I think it is just as well not to think about things like that too much'."

From "This Is My Story," by Eleanor Roosevelt.

". . . That is why," said Franklin Roosevelt in the commencement address at Milton Academy, Massachusetts, in 1926, "I sympathize little with those radicals who tell me that our religion is dead, that our government is basically wrong. The churches today are beginning to go along with the new scientific growth and are opening the way to a simpler faith, a deeper faith, a *happier* faith, than ever our forefathers held."

69

VESTRY ROOM OF ST. JAMES CHURCH.

70

Just east of the State Road and south of "Springwood's" gateposts you
can see Mrs. James Roosevelt's barns, the farm, where the cattle and
chickens were.

Franklin helped his mother in running the farm. They kept a large account
book in which they recorded what was being done. On one page of this book is
a map carefully drawn by F.D.R. showing the roads, the farm buildings and the
positions of the various fields, and naming them, "south lot," "wood lot," etc.
On the opposite and succeeding pages are listed the amount of the particular crop
grown and harvested on each field, with other pertinent remarks.

*   *   *

"When at Hyde Park tomorrow, I will go over the locations for planting
the 8,000 trees, and also see how they are getting on with the clearing for
new pastures.

Much love from us both,
Ever your affectionate
F.D.R."

*From a letter by F.D.R. to Sara Delano Roosevelt, sent
from the Senate of the State of New York, March 17, 1912.*

Golf was another sport that was indulged in by the River families. As we've already seen, the Rogers had their own small links. Even my grandfather had three holes on "Glenburn's" two available fields, for in those days of moving by carriage, it was quite a trip to go five miles for a game. At Staatsburg, New York, the Ogden Mills and the William Dinsmores built a small course; it was one of the first in this country. Between them, they kept it in excellent condition. They invited a number of the neighbors to join their very private enterprise. It was never referred to as a club, but it was the nearest thing to one our community has ever had. Some twenty miles to the north, Tivoli has supported an active tennis and golf club that even indulges in activities as sociable as tournaments and lunches. Much later, Red Hook founded a flourishing golf club to satisfy the active demand of many local enthusiasts. The Staatsburg links looks now much as it did when F.D.R. played there with Lydig Hoyt or other neighbors and guests. One section of the Dinsmore barns, with their picturesque four-leaf-clover windows, shows in the background of the picture.

"He stayed (in North East Harbor) a week, having a wonderful time, dancing, renewing acquaintances, and playing what was then considered a new-fangled game called golf.

"So impressed was he with this sport that he determined to introduce it on our little island (Campobello). With zeal and hard labor worthy of a better cause, he charted out the first links ever built there and put them into the best shape possible."

From "My Boy Franklin".

SILVER CUPS WON BY FRANKLIN ROOSEVELT FOR GOLF AND ICE BOATING.

With his amazing versatility, F.D.R. enjoyed almost all sports, and he had many hobbies. As a very small boy he was a regular exhibitor at the Dutchess County Fair. One gets the feeling that after childhood he liked horses more for locomotion than for sport, but he continued to show at the fair's horse show, which was then held in Poughkeepsie. Now it takes place in our town, Rhinebeck. When he was Governor and also when he was President, Mr. Roosevelt would always motor up for a visit if he could find time. The fair is the most important yearly event in our county's social life. On every child's horizon it ranks with the circus and Christmas. It is a meeting place for all groups. Here the dignity and importance of the farmer's product are publicly recognized. It has become the local mecca for the trotting races, which in James Roosevelt's day were run frequently at the Union Corners race track in Hyde Park, and at other tracks throughout the State. These trotting races have a country flavor, and arouse a local interest which the far more celebrated and fashionable horse races never achieve.

"Prior to F.D.R.'s nomination for State Senator," Judge John E. Mack writes, "he took no part in Dutchess County politics. I went to see him with some papers from his father's estate, I then being in the office of John Hackett (the Hyde Park lawyer who took care of James Roosevelt's affairs). The two Chanler boys (Robert Chanler, the painter, 'Sheriff Bob,' and Lewis Stuyvesant Chanler, member of the State Assembly) I thought, were tiring of Dutchess County, and while talking to Mr. Roosevelt in Carter, Ledyard and Milburn's office, it seemed to me he would make a good candidate for the Assembly. He was interested, and during that summer I took him around to clam bakes and other places. I suggested that he talk with Lewis Stuyvesant Chanler, Assemblyman, to see if Mr. Chanler would

74

not run for Congress or State Senator. Mr. Chanler felt sure of being elected to the Assembly but not to the Senate or Congress. He very politely declined to run for any other office. F.D.R. reported this to me. I then suggested that he run for the Senate. There was one chance in five of his success. He unhesitatingly said he would run, but inquired as to the probability of his obtaining the nomination. I told him the nomination was made by a Committee that year, of which I was one member, and quite sure of the other two."

This committee duly nominated Franklin Roosevelt. Judge Mack, who was then District Attorney of Dutchess County, offered the resolution endorsing Mr. Roosevelt for State Senator at the county convention in Poughkeepsie on October 6. This left only four weeks for an intensive campaign. However, during the summer John Mack had taken Franklin Roosevelt to clam bakes and other social events around the county so the voters would get to know him. As in the case of so many patterns that recur in F.D.R.'s life, it was John Mack, who nominated him for President at the Democratic Convention in the Chicago Stadium on June 30, 1932.

75

In his speech accepting this first nomination, Mr. Roosevelt said: "As you know, I accept the nomination with absolute independence. I am pledged to no man, I am influenced by no specific interests, and so I shall remain."

*   *   *

"He went back to the campaign, a novel campaign, for no one had ever before tried visiting every small four-corner store and every village and every town. He took the other candidates with him and they went by motor with a delightful character named Hawkey whom we were to know quite well during the next four years. We owned no car ourselves at that time, so Franklin hired Hawkey and his car. There was no top on the car as I remember it, but they drove all over the district, rain or shine . . .

"He (Franklin), spoke slowly, and every now and then there would be a long pause, and I would be worried for fear he would never go on . . ."

From "This Is My Story," by Eleanor Roosevelt.

The local Republican politicians were amused by the thought of this green candidate's campaigning in a car. They were sure he didn't have a chance. No Democrat had. The rural districts were traditionally Republican; moreover, the farmers hated motor cars. This rarely seen new-fangled contraption spread devastation in the barn yard and terrified horses along the road.

The opposition politicians were less pleased, however, when they realized how effective Franklin Roosevelt's careful behavior was. For, when he saw a team approaching, he stopped both his car and the engine. This gave him the opportunity to say a few words to the passing farmer and to drive home the two main points he made in the campaign: The boss-ridden quality of the local Republican Party and his own considerate interest in the farmer. He had become actively aware of the unfairness of the farmer's lot through the disintegration of a neighboring family, a hardworking family with four children, such as comprise the backbone of a community. When the parents died and two children married, the remaining boy and girl ran the farm. Misfortune and illness came with age. The mortgage was foreclosed, and the family, who deserved well of their community, ended up in the poor house.

*   *   *

"I want to go back for a minute to the old days before I got to know the United States," said F.D.R. in an extemporaneous speech at Vassar College, on August 26, 1933. "It is, I think, just twenty-three years ago that I chanced to be in Poughkeepsie on a Saturday morning in August, a very hot Saturday morning.

"In front of the court house, I ran across a group of friends of mine. As I remember, they were Judge Morschauser, George Spratt, John Mack, and Judge Arnold. I had only intended to stay in town for a few minutes to do some errands, but they kidnaped me — one of the first cases of deliberate kidnaping on record — and took me out to the policemen's picnic in Fairview.

THE OLD RED MAXWELL.

"On that joyous occasion of clams and sauerkraut and real beer I made my first speech, and I have been apologizing for it ever since.

"And also on that same occasion I started to make the acquaintance of that part of Dutchess County that lies outside of the town of Hyde Park.

"And I continued to make that acquaintance all through the campaign that year, although in August I hadn't the foggiest idea that I was going to run for the State Senate; and it was only because another band of kidnapers kidnaped me that I got into public life at all

"For I had to talk, and I was given the opportunity of making the acquaintance of a county.

77

"And today, as I drive along a beautiful concrete highway, or one of the new county roads, I see in my mind's eye that same road as it existed in the autumn of 1910 as I proceeded over it at the dangerous pace of about twenty-two miles an hour in Mr. Hawkey's old red Maxwell, without any front windshield, without any top — an old Maxwell, that, when we met a horse or a team — and that was about every half mile or so — we had to stop, not only the car, but the engine as well."

* * *

He covered much of our county, as this typical day's schedule, dated October 25, 1910, shows: He stopped at the railroad stations in Patterson; Holmes; West Pawling, and Stormville. The picture shows him chatting at a mill between Poughquag (where he spoke at Frank Brill's store) and Beekman (here he spoke at the general store). The last stop on this day's Dutchess County electioneering was at Hopewell Junction. There he addressed a large evening meeting in the hall.

Most of his political conferences took place in his small study which looks out on the front terrace. In the illustration above, he is talking with John Mack, John Townsend, and John Sague, all local Democratic leaders. The last-named became Mayor of Poughkeepsie. Judge Mack has achieved a national reputation as lawyer, judge, and able leader in the Democratic Party.

"Roosevelt's own study at Hyde Park was always a little room off the back hall. It had been his study as a boy, and it was 'plenty good enough for me' when he was Governor. He liked it just that way. The room was small, the desk big. He had a comfortable old chair, a few knick knacks, and the books he wanted near by. 'Everything right within reach', he would say cheerfully."

From "The Roosevelt I Knew," by Frances Perkins.

During 1914 the plans for lifting the face of the Hyde Park house were
started. The family wanted more space for living. Also Franklin Roosevelt's
political career, his continuous collecting, and his numerous other activities,
made larger downstairs rooms desirable. We have seen the earlier appearance
of the house as a background to a goat cart, and also as it looked from the
southwest, in the picture of the two Roosevelt houses. Its comfortable Victorian
front gave way to the present, more impressive facade. Its new look was
completed in 1915 under the supervison of the architect, Francis L. V. Hoppin.

"Every house with which he has been identified has been reproduced in
a miniature model, so accurately, for all its tiny scale, that it is really a work
of art. When we remodeled the home at Hyde Park, it used to be much
smaller and dated from a period when American architecture was not at its

best; he participated eagerly in every detail of the planning. We flung out a wing at each end, took off old-fashioned porches which darkened the ground floor rooms, and made a graceful, round portico and central entrance, sacrificing a squat, ugly tower for deep windows and an outdoor play-roof for the babies. Franklin constructed, in a most ingenious little model, the whole 'new' house as we visioned it in our long family talks by the open fire."

From "My Boy Franklin"

The life-size bronze, shown below, was modeled by Prince Paul Troubetskoy when F.D.R. was twenty-eight. The sculptor wanted to do a full-length figure, standing or seated, but finally truncated it, saying that he "couldn't see Franklin Roosevelt with legs."

"He looked thin then, tall, high-strung, and, at times, nervous. White skin and fair hair, deep-set blue eyes and clear-cut features. No lines as yet in his face, but at times the set look of his jaw denoted that this apparently pliable youth had strength and Dutch obstinacy in his make-up."

From "This Is My Story," by Eleanor Roosevelt.

Franklin Roosevelt got his first pony when he was seven. From then on he did much riding, with his father, then with his mother, later with his own wife and children. They would go out together, over the dirt roads and bridle paths that cover the place. In this picture we see Anna and James on their own horses, while baby Elliott is perched on the front of his father's saddle. They are riding on their private road that connects Route 9-G with Route 9. The latter is flanked by a superb alley of large maple trees, some of which show in the picture and about which President Roosevelt wrote the following memorandum to J. S. Bixby, divisional engineer of the State Highways Department:

"In about 1740, John Crook lived in a stone house, just east of where my brother, J. R. Roosevelt's house now stands (the Red House). Crook's son who knew the place and loved the country, lost his eyes in an accident but continued to live there and though blind, planted the wonderful row of trees on each side of the Post Road from the top of Teller's Hill and probably up as far as the Rogers' farm. It is an interesting fact that many of these original trees, now 200 years old, are still standing. Ever since then, for every tree that has fallen down or been struck by lightening, another tree has been planted. There is nothing quite like it anywhere in America."

Throughout his life Franklin Roosevelt added to his various collections. For example, this model of the *Constitution*, which was made in the Washington Navy Yard shortly after the War of 1812, was bought by F.D.R. in 1914. He considered it to be his best model. Some of the collection was housed in the new wing, some stayed in the rented Washington house, or one of the family New York houses. Although his acquisitions of naval material constitute the most important part of his collections, he was also buying much material relating to family and local history and making a small collection of chap, miniature, and children's books.

From his introduction to political life in 1910, he was working in Albany as State Senator, in New York in various business, charitable, and social activities, and later, from 1913 to 1920, in Washington as Assistant Secretary of the Navy. The family was completed with the birth of John in 1916. Louis Howe, correspondent for *The New York Herald* in Albany, became a member of Roosevelt's circle, and his most important political adviser. In 1912, when

F.D.R. was in bed with typhoid, Howe ran the successful State Senatorial campaign which he won by five hundred votes, a larger majority than F.D.R. had on his initial election. "Springwood" remained the background for much of the family life and for many of F.D.R.'s avocations, and for the country sports which he kept up and taught his children whenever he had the time. It was also the scene of a number of political conferences such as the important "get-together" of Democratic leaders from Dutchess, Orange, Putnam, and Columbia Counties, who met there on June 5, 1920.

As Assistant Secretary of the Navy during the First World War, F.D.R. was away most of the time; away in Washington with administrative work and making official speeches; away on inspection trips abroad and in the United States. This early part of his career was climaxed by his nomination for the Vice Presidency in 1920 by the Democratic party.

Franklin Roosevelt was now placed squarely on the national scene. So, to help the Roosevelts to cope with the accumulated correspondence left over from Washington as well as with the new influx, result of the Vice Presidential campaign, the Democratic National Committe lent Miss Marguerite LeHand to the family. As Louis Howe had become earlier, "Missy" became a permanent member of the political and family circle. A third member of that circle, of which she is still so important a part, Miss Malvina Thompson, "Tommy," became Mrs. Roosevelt's secretary at about this time.

NAVAL COLLECTION BOOKPLATE DESIGNED BY F.D.R.

On July 13, 1920, when Mr. Roosevelt returned from the convention, he was met at the Poughkeepsie station by crowds and waving flags. Several hundred persons and the village band were at his gate. They formed a procession, and escorted the nominee to his house. There, former State Senator Thomas Newbold presented him to the crowd on the drive with this introduction, "Here's our boy!"

"Neighbors, I am more moved by this than by anything else in my life," the candidate said. "I am more moved than I was at San Francisco when the unexpected happened . . .

"I want to tell you from the bottom of my heart that my success is due to my association with the good old stock of Dutchess County and the straight-thinking people I have been brought up among here. That has given me the inspiration to do everything I've done . . .

"About the first of August, a most extraordinary thing is going to happen here. They are going to notify me of my nomination for the Vice Presidency and my strongest inclination is that I'll accept. The leaders of the national party will be here, but the thing that will count most will be your presence. I hope you will be here to help me through with it. I need all the help I can get. I don't mean votes. I mean your moral support.

"There is one thing that I want to tell you and that is that the National Democratic Convention was run in the open. All my life I have tried to do things in the open, where everyone could see and where nothing was concealed. That was the spirit of the convention, and I hope it will be the spirit of the campaign. I hope that there will be no mud-slinging and that the issues will be presented fully, clearly and honestly."

Henry Morgenthau, Jr., arranged for the formal notification on August 9, when 5,000 came to "Springwood" to hear F.D.R.'s acceptance speech. Here the nominee came out strongly for international coöperation, the League of Nations, internal reform, and reorganization of the governmental machinery.

On this occasion, I remember that Mrs. James Roosevelt was annoyed and refused to rekiss her son for the news photographers who had missed getting the photograph as he came up the steps.

"This notification meeting was the first really mammoth meeting to be held at Hyde Park. This gathering was the predecessor of many others, but I sympathized with my mother-in-law when I saw her lawn being trampled by hordes of people. My admiration for her has grown through the years as I realized how many political guests she has had to entertain in her house, where for so many years, only family and friends were received."

From "This Is My Story," by Eleanor Roosevelt.

In November, despite an arduous campaign by F.D.R., the returns as they were received at "Springwood" indicated that the country had chosen to return to "normalcy" and had elected Harding and Coolidge. But his political and business activity continued during the winter following his defeat. Early in August he cruised up to Campobello for a rest.

On August 10, 1921, after a particularly active day, which included putting out a forest fire and taking a dip in the ocean, he caught a severe chill. The resulting illness was diagnosed, too late, as infantile paralysis.

This terrace, seen through two of the front portico columns, has been the stage for some of F.D.R.'s greatest scenes, as well as many of his quieter ones. He accepted the Vice Presidential nomination here, and here he always received the election-night parade of the Roosevelt Club of Hyde Park. During his illness he'd spend much time sitting on the terrace or under the portico, working while he could look out at the front lawn's handsome trees and remember that as a child he had climbed in the branches of the great fir on the left of the picture.

Franklin Roosevelt spent the first winter of his illness in New York City. His mother expected him to retire to Hyde Park and indulge his hobby of writing history, but his wife and his doctor, George Draper, agreed that he should not retire. While still on his back he wrote in his own hand a card catalogue of his naval book collections, with notes on date of purchase and price paid, and with comments as to rarity. He continued with most of his civic and business interests. People came to see him, and he kept up a voluminous and catholic correspondence. In the spring, he moved up to Hyde Park, and for the following seven years lived there, in New York City, and at Warm Springs, Georgia. It was then that Mrs. Franklin Roosevelt really entered political life. She and Louis Howe kept F.D.R.'s name before the public. In August, 1924, he held an important and publicized conference with John W. Davis, Al Smith and other leaders of the party, at Hyde Park. In 1925 he wrote a series of political articles for the *Macon (Georgia) Daily Telegram*, and another series in 1928 for the *Beacon (New York) Standard* called "Between Neighbors." At the 1924 Democratic convention he made his famous "Happy Warrior" speech nominating Al Smith. This was the first time his voice was heard on a nation-wide radio hook up.

However, the part of his life with which this book is concerned is that spent here in Hyde Park. I've suggested some aspects of that daily routine, in the pictures that immediately follow. He would be pushed in his wheel

ONE OF THE CARDS WRITTEN BY F.D.R.
FOR HIS NAVAL BOOK COLLECTION FILE.

89

chair around the grounds, usually by Robert McGaughey, for many years his mother's house man and butler. Often he'd go to see the "Rosy" Roosevelts, passing the children's playhouse on the way.

* * *

"The only acknowledgment I have found that it meant anything to him personally is this: in a warning to a newspaper man in 1928 which was evidentally not intended for publication:

" 'Now, I don't want any sob-stuff in the relation of my experience. Of course it was a great shock to be stricken down at a time when, except for natural exhaustion after a hard campaign, I felt myself to be in the pink of condition. And it was rather humiliating to contract a disease of which 75 per cent of the victims are children. But I am thankful that my children were spared'."

From "Franklin D. Roosevelt," by Ernest K. Lindley.

A path was put down skirting the lawn from the turn-around to the dirt road that joins "Springwood" to the "Red House." Its direction can still be followed in the grass. On this path F.D.R.'s chair could more easily be pushed along. The rhythm of the trees as you walk along this path is particularly attractive. He knew the place well as a boy. During these years he must have learned to know it even better.

Often, F.D.R. and Louis Howe would sit under the portico or on the terrace in front of his office door and make sail-boat models. Howe would usually work on the drawings and F.D.R. carve the hulls.

Mrs. Roosevelt writes illuminating passages about Louis Howe in her book, *This Is My Story*:

"Mr. Howe had made up his mind to give up all idea of taking the position which was open to him and to come back to his old boss, because he saw quite plainly that his help was going to be needed. From that time on, he put his whole heart into working for my husband's future.

"Ever since the Albany days, he had been a very intimate friend and co-worker of my husband's. At times, I resented this intimacy, and at this time I was very sure of my own judgment about people. I frequently tried to influence those about me, and there were occasions when I thought that Louis Howe's influence and mine, where my husband was concerned, had clashed; and I was, of course, sure I was right . . .

"In later years, I learned that he had always liked me and thought I

was worth educating, and for that reason, he made an effort on this trip (the 1920 campaign) to get to know me . . .

"Louis Howe began to break down my antagonisms by occasionally knocking at my stateroom door and asking if he might discuss a speech with me. I was flattered, and before long I found myself discussing a wide range of subjects. I began to be able to understand some of our newspaper brethren, and to look upon them as friends instead of enemies."

*   *   *

Mr. Roosevelt's pleasure in making things with his large but sensitively controlled hands stood him in good stead now. He'd work for hours sorting and pasting stamps without the help of stamp tongs, although this procedure is frowned upon by philatelists. As an amateur carpenter, he made many objects, among them a bookcase of mahogany-stained cherry wood for his mother. Especially he enjoyed designing and executing model sail boats with Louis Howe, and with Ralph Cropley, who sometimes visited Hyde Park. He, Louis Howe, and F.D.R. made between them twenty-seven models to sail across the Hudson. One of F.D.R.'s *Crum Elbows* made the record crossing in fifteen minutes. Louis Howe had a whole series of *Horse's Necks*. There were semi-annual races in the spring for the Roosevelt Cup and in the fall for the Hyde Park Cup. These races usually took place from the "Rosedale" boat house; each model was followed by a rowboat. At other times, F.D.R. would sail his own models from the railroad siding below the house.

From the turn-around in front of the house to the brownstone gate posts on Route 9, it is more than a quarter of a mile of gravelled road, flanked by a double row of maple trees. One of the exercises prescribed by the doctor was for Mr. Roosevelt to walk with his crutches down this drive; a little further each day, until he finally reached the entrance. Later, he confessed that the effort put into these walks was a terrible strain, that he permanently injured some of his leg muscles and in all probability his heart also.

"All that summer at Hyde Park, my husband struggled to do a great number of things which would make it possible for him to be more active. He learned to use crutches and walked every day to gain confidence. Each new thing he did took not only determination but great physical effort."

From "This Is My Story," by Eleanor Roosevelt.

* * *

With the family seated around, he exercised on the south lawn. There were parallel bars, also rings, as shown in the picture, and the platform

96

described by Mrs. Charles Hamlin in her article in *The New Republic*,
April 15, 1946: "One of his knees had locked, and he was carrying through
a program of very rigid exercises trying to improve the condition. I watched
as he made his endless rounds, for two or three hours a day, holding on
to the wooden railing of a rectangular walk. Usually, several of his friends
were sitting around, and he talked and laughed cheerfully as he circled the
platform, holding himself up by the railing and dragging his almost useless
legs after him."

*　　*　　*

When I was doing the Hyde Park post-office murals, the President
told me to look at the woods below the house, as they would suggest a
background for the early panels. Here is the entrance gateway to this primeval
forest. At one time, the rustic fence was more elaborate, and there was a fine
gate, entrance to this large stand of untimbered land which is unique in our

county. As you remember, F.D.R. was proud of it and interested in it. He hoped the primeval forest would be left to grow for all time, without cutting or trimming.

* * *

Often, between 1921 and 1926, the whole family would swim in the pond in these same woods below the house — the very same pond where, as a little boy, he went fishing and watching the men cut ice. Now F.D.R. would sit on the dam and let himself into the water. Louis Depew, Mrs. James Roosevelt's coachman and later her chauffeur, taught the children to swim. Here, he has one of them on the end of the fish pole.

* * *

F.D.R. was sociable. He frequently drove to see his neighbors in and around Hyde Park, men and women he had known since his childhood. We see him visiting Benjamin Haviland, one of his oldest friends who lives on Route 9-G, not far north of "Val-Kill" (a piece of land we shall discuss a little later). Sometimes F.D.R. would sit in the car, which was specially designed so that he could drive it himself.

Not more than a mile south of Uncle Ben Haviland's farm was the one F.D.R. rented to Moses Smith. Here, too, he would come and chat. Later, this house achieved considerable celebrity, for the Roosevelt Home Club, a local political organization, which was started in 1929, met on its lawn from 1934 on. The Home Club also inaugurated the annual birthday ball in the town hall in 1929, which grew into the great series of annual balls that covered the nation, and whose proceeds were given to The National Foundation for Infantile Paralysis.

There was much to learn from the way his neighbors were thinking and talking, for they usually expressed their ideas in colorful and emphatic language. It's this conscious knowledge of his neighbors which becomes so apparent when

one reads these notes which the President made for the Dutchess County Historical Society year book, concerning his first "Fireside Chat":

"The imperative purposes would not be answered unless it (the speech) was understood and approved by the type of individual whom I thought of as the 'average depositor' (of the banks). This caused me to sit down at my desk and try to visualize the types representative of the majority. I tried to picture a mason, a girl behind a counter, and a farmer in his field. Perhaps my thoughts went back to this land of individual citizens whom I have known so well in Dutchess County all my life."

*   *   *

At the welcome-home meeting on Moses Smith's lawn in August, 1934, F.D.R. told his neighbors:

". . . The more we shall realize that if a farm family is on the verge of starvation in North Dakota, we people in the town of Hyde Park are helping to pay to keep that family from actual starvation; if we have made mistakes in the settling of the country in the past, we in the town of Hyde Park have to pay to correct those mistakes. In other words, we should realize that we have a definite stake in the whole country, not merely the spiritual side of it, or the social side of it, or the patriotic side, but the actual financial side of it. We people in the town of Hyde Park, no matter whether we like it or not, are paying, and will have to pay, for the correction of mistakes that were made in other parts of the country in the past, and will have to pay to get things better."

In the informal remarks on election night, November 4, 1941, at Hyde Park, part of which are printed below, the President discussed with his neighbors his interest in government planning. He felt that democracy should start planning intelligently in the township, and that the success and caliber of national planning was in fact dependent on the results achieved on this lower level of government.

". . . The town is growing so fast, and there are so many new problems being presented to us from time to time, that in the long run it will pay us if we plan. And at the same time, when we do something, it will be in accordance with an effort to guess into the future, and do things that we won't have to re-do because of failure to plan ahead."

F.D.R. bought, from time to time, pieces of land which he added to his own farm and on which he experimented, especially in the growing of trees. He operated his land as a productive farm, in contradistinction to the views of his mother, for she had insisted that her place be run as it had been when James Roosevelt was alive. At "Val-Kill," which means "valley stream" in Dutch, F.D.R. made most of these plantations, with the advice of the State Conservation Department at the Syracuse College of Forestry. Among other trees, you will find European larch, Scotch pine and Dahurian larch from Korea. From both the natural wood lots on the farm and from these plantations he sold cross-ties, telegraph poles, pilings, saw logs and cord wood. During the war, he timbered the largest wood lot for shipbuilding. "Forest operations on a farm of this sort," he said, "can and should be used to meet the entire tax burden levied against the property." Though he loved the trees for themselves, he also thought of them as an asset to a working farm.

Mr. Roosevelt got the greatest fun out of his plantations of Norway spruce, Douglas fir and other varieties, popularly known as Christmas trees. The low hills east of 9-G are dotted with them, and F.D.R. would drive all over these hills and their miles of dirt road. Often he would watch while seedling Christmas trees were planted. In this procedure, a line is stretched across the field. Then a group of men with pails of seedlings and shovels, following the tape, plant the trees at two-yard intervals. These first Christmas-

tree plantings started in 1925. It takes at least ten years for the trees to mature, and then only a limited number of the largest ones are ready to harvest. In the picture, William Plog, head foreman and gardener who came to the Roosevelts when he was a boy of sixteen, is seen talking to Mr. Roosevelt and supervising the planting.

In 1936, the first year the Christmas trees were ready for cutting, F.D.R. was as pleased as a child with a new toy. He went out himself, to choose a number of special ones for the family and a few friends. He could not wait

to have them cut and sent off to their destinations. As a business venture, the trees turned out very well. Except for the initial planting and the eventual cutting, they need little attention, and grow well on relatively poor soil. When cut, the trees were stacked at the "Val-Kill Farms," near the Roosevelt High School. In the picture, a child is negotiating with Mr. Plog for the purchase of a tree, while another child is hauling his purchase home. Most of the business, however, was wholesale.

Farther to the south on this same piece of land, there is a charming birch grove through which the "Val-Kill" stream flows. A small pond was made by damming the stream. It had always been a favorite picnic place for the family. In 1925, Mrs. Roosevelt and three friends decided to build a stone cottage with a swimming pool. F.D.R., pleased with the idea, sketched a plan and Henry Toombs, Atlanta architect, made the blueprints. When the contracting estimates came in and were deemed too high, Mr. Roosevelt undertook the job himself; found a carpenter and mason, and was delighted when he could hand over the finished building with several thousand dollars saved over the original estimates. In an adjoining building Mrs. Roosevelt started a furniture factory for hand-made early American pieces. When the factory was discontinued she used the building as her home. She lives there now.

* * *

Boating, like swimming and picnics, was one of the activities the whole family enjoyed doing together. Here we see them near the "Rosedale" boat house, about 1912, sailing model boats that F.D.R. had made. Mrs. Roosevelt is pushing one rowboat away from the bank, F.D.R. is at the oars of another, with Anna in the stern; Elliott is guiding his boat with a stick — while John plays on the rocks with a tiny boat, and Mr. and Mrs. "Rosy" Roosevelt look on from the shore.

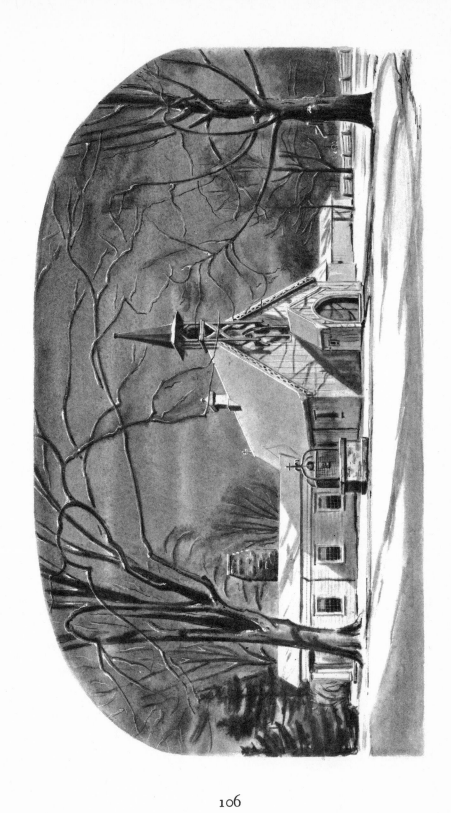

106

When St. James Church is closed in winter from December to March, the Roosevelts go to St. James Chapel in the village. This chapel is a graceful example of "pig-sty Gothic." The oldest part of the building, in the Classic Revival style of 1832, was used as a school until 1856, when the chapel was built. Now it is the parish house.

"Unfortunately, of course, although our own township dates back for nearly two hundred and fifty years," the President said at the Methodist Episcopal Church at Hyde Park, on September 29, 1933, "the religious life of this particular community did not begin in an organized way until after the Revolution. Before that time, there wasn't any Hyde Park. There was a district of the County of Dutchess that was known as 'the Krum Elbow Precinct' and across Krum Elbow Creek there was a country place that belonged to Dr. John Bard that was known as Hyde Park. But this community, until after the Revolution, went by various names, among others as DeCantillon's Landing and Stoutenbergh's Store . . .

"It was not until 1789 that the people in this community who belonged to various churches got together and decided that they ought to have a meeting house; and thus in 1789 there was organized the Stoutenbergh Religious Society, an association of men and women who wanted a place in which to worship. As a result, there was put up the first church and what afterwards became the Hyde Park Building. I suppose it was a very tiny structure, because it seated only forty-eight persons; but the interesting thing about that church in 1789 was that at the meeting of the people who organized it, a resolution was passed which said that the church shall be open to every good and well-recommended preacher and to every Christian society. In other words, it was a church for all of the divisions of the Protestant faith. There were not many

Baptists here in those days, they tell us, but there were Methodists, there were Dutch Reform followers, there were Presbyterians and Protestant Episcopalians and, for a number of years — in fact, for a whole generation — this entire community worshiped in this house of the Religious Society.

"A generation later, in 1811, the Protestant Episcopal Church was organized; and then there came the Methodist Episcopal Church . . .

"My own association with this church goes back to a very, very early period, in the early eighties.

"I remember one day, on my way home, I passed a little house that was occupied by that splendid old couple, Mr. and Mrs. John Clay, and Mrs. John Clay invited me in to give me a piece of gingerbread; and that was when I discovered that there was another church in the village besides my own. So Mrs. Clay was responsible for my first association with Methodism, and it was done with a piece of gingerbread . . .

"It is not only the spirit of these times, but it seems to me that it is fundamentally a matter of common sense, that in our religious worship we should work together instead of flying off on different tangents and different angles, pulling apart instead of pulling together as a unified whole. During these later years there has been a splendid change for the better in this regard. We find today the ministers of the different churches sitting amicably side by side on the same platform. More than that, we find them meeting with each other from time to time to try to help solve the community problems together."

HAVING LUNCH WITH LOUIS HOWE ON THE WEST PORCH.

"You probably know of Father's custom of reading Dickens' *Christmas Carol* to the assembled family on the last couple of evenings before Christmas. I remember Father in his chair before the burning fire in the big library surrounded by children and adults alike, some on the floor as well as on the sofa and chairs, listening while he read. His facial expressions while imitating Mr. Scrooge were quite fearsome to the young!"

From a letter by Mrs. John Boettiger, daughter of F.D.R.

The painting above the fireplace is Gilbert Stuart's portrait of Isaac Roosevelt who, as you will remember, was F.D.R.'s great great grandfather.

The remodeling of "Springwood," the designing of "Val-Kill Cottage" and this, the James Roosevelt Memorial Library (built 1926) on the main street of Hyde Park village, exemplify Franklin Roosevelt's interest in our early Dutch builders and their local material, fieldstone. Shortly, his taste was to influence the design of all new public buildings in Hyde Park.

At the dedication of the Rhinebeck post office, on May 1, 1939, President Roosevelt said: "We are seeking to follow the type of architecture which is good in the sense that it does not of necessity follow the whims of the moment but seeks an artistry that ought to be good, as far as we can tell, for all time to come . . ."

I do not share Mr. Roosevelt's enthusiasm for this form of archaeological designing, but I do not doubt that the public buildings produced in our

community under his influence are vastly superior to those produced by our communities' recent taste when left to its own devices.

The whole matter of the President's feeling for fieldstone had a curious result in our strongly Republican town of Rhinebeck. One afternoon he drove Princess Juliana of the Netherlands, who was visiting his family at "Springwood," to look at the site which the Rhinebeck school board and the qualified voters of the district had selected for their new centralized school building. Mr. Roosevelt and the members of the school board discussed the site chosen, but there was no mention of materials because the plot plan had not been drawn, or the architects selected. Yet the rumor got around that the President had come up, selected the site, and insisted that the new school be built of fieldstone. This gossip added materially to the difficulties in getting the community to vote for a much needed building.

*   *   *

This concern with our Dutch architecture was only one aspect of the interest Franklin Roosevelt took in history generally and in local history in particular. His conversation was full of personal and historical reminiscences, as well as facts and stories about local history. He lived in the stream of history. He talked about Jefferson as if the third President had been one of his grandfathers. He felt the past of the United States, as well as that of Dutchess County, as if it were his own immediate past.

During these years, he and Miss Helen W. Reynolds, the most active member of the Dutchess County Historical Society (which he had joined on its founding in 1914) drove all over the county examining tombstones and records, locating historic sites, discovering and visiting old houses.

In 1923 he purchased the original *Minutes of Council of Appointment of New York at Poughkeepsie in 1778-1779*, and by arrangement with the New York Historical Society published it in an edition limited to fifty copies. He also helped to publish, as part of the collection of the Dutchess County Historical Society, two books by Miss Reynolds, and *The Records of the Town of Hyde Park* edited by himself. He also edited *Vessels of Fishkill During the Revolution* for the society year book, and he served as town historian from 1926 until well into his second term as Governor, in 1931. The last official letter he wrote to the State Historian requests the appointment of Benjamin Haviland as his successor as historian for the town of Hyde Park.

The annual pilgrimage of the Dutchess County Historical Society met on the Roosevelt lawn, on September 16, 1927. According to the report in the year book, he discussed the Hyde Park patent of 1697, and the "Great Nine Partners' Patent" and what the ownership of land in fee simple, or absolute ownership, meant to the development of the community.

F.D.R.'s application of the lessons of the past to the problems of the present — in this case, architecture and the decorative arts — is suggested in his introduction to Miss Reynolds' book, *Pre-Revolutionary Dutch Homes*: ". . . We are concerned, however, not merely as antiquarians. The architecture, the decorations, the furniture of our early settlers have a very definite relationship to the arts of today. It is true that our modern life calls for conveniences unthought of in Seventeenth-century New Amsterdam, but the charm of line, the judgment of location, and the spirit of simplicity of the homes of our ancestors, are all a good influence on a civilization which to some of us seems to be reverting to the more humble and honest ideals."

Of course, his primary interest was not architecture or the decorative arts. It was politics. During these years of enforced contemplation, the formal expression of his political philosophy became simpler and clearer. It was exemplified in speeches and articles, among others a talk to the graduating class of 1926 at Milton Academy in Massachusetts, in which he said: "Unrest in this world of ours is caused as much by those who fear changes as by those who seek revolution; and unrest in any nation or in any organization, whether it be caused by ultra-conservatism or by extreme radicalism, is in the long run a healthy sign. In government, in science, in industry, in the arts, inaction and apathy are the most potent foes."

He knew that people wanted security above all else, and he felt that "security should be the main aim of government today; the arguments should be about ways and means."

Although he enjoyed his hobby of history as many men enjoy golf, for relaxation and entertainment, it also had an obviously profound effect on his thinking and on the way in which he expressed his thoughts. As Archibald MacLeish wrote in *The New Republic* of April 15, 1946: "Mr. Roosevelt approached the culture of Americans as he approached their political life and their economic and social institutions, as an historian or, rather, as a political leader whose intellectual preoccupation was history . . . The sense of history in a political leader is a sense of the past as the past has meaning for the future. The sense of posterity is a presence in the earth. And to any man who feels it, learning and the arts are the continuing realities."

Mr. Roosevelt's talk to the Daughters of the American Revolution at their national convention on April 21, 1938, affords a good example of his application of history to the political issues of his own day:

"I thought of preaching on a text, but I shall not. I shall only give you the text, and I shall not preach on it. I think I can afford to give you the text because it so happens, through no fault of my own, that I am descended from a number of people who came over on the *Mayflower*. More than that, every one of my ancestors on both sides — and when you go back four or five generations it means thirty-two or sixty-four of them — every single one of them, without exception, was in this land in 1776, and there was only one Tory among them.

"The text is this: Remember, remember always that all of us, and you and I especially, are descended from immigrants and revolutionists."

During his Governorship, F.D.R. had fieldstone protections built around the red sandstone road markers put up every mile between New York and Albany sometime before 1774. This one is just south of the "Springwood" entrance gates.

Every Governor of New York State gets his official chair for each term he serves. One of these large chairs stands on each side of the fireplace in the library. F.D.R. used to sit on the one at the left; there he would mix cocktails before dinner.

*   *   *

Happy and enthusiastic as he was in his public career — in his many outside interests and in new friends and acquaintances — his family, his home, his old friends, and the countryside in which he had his roots, all these became, not less, but more important to him as he grew older. He rarely missed a chance to stop on his way to or from Albany for lunch, tea, or dinner or a weekend with his mother at Hyde Park. He was continually drawn there, as a study of the diaries, letters and even the date-lines in news

116

stories makes abundantly clear. Like his father, he, his children and grand-children lived in the same house, played under the same woods, rode over the same paths. That he could come back here from either Albany or Washington rested him and gave him strength.

After he had been elected Governor, he said to a friend: "Anyway, I'm going to retire at fifty. I think I will have done my duty to the public by then, don't you? There are so many things I want to do here, in Hyde Park, as a private citizen." This kind of remark may have been prompted by the fact that one side of him was reluctant to reenter political life. For by the end of 1928 he had seen signs of improvement in his legs, and he believed that another two years of treatment would make their use possible. But while he was staying at Warm Springs, Al Smith drafted him by telephone to head the State Democratic ticket. By taking on this job, he gave up all hope of regaining the use of his legs.

*　　*　　*

A chronological list of the important events which occured at Hyde Park from 1928 on would cover many pages. It was the scene of vital conferences. Announcements of international significance were date-lined from here. F.D.R. delivered a surprising number of speeches locally, and broadcast two major and several minor speeches from his office in the library. To tell what discussions and decisions were made in the course of lunches at "Top Cottage," picnics in the county, afternoon swims at "Val-Kill," drives in the blue Ford, or talks in the small study at the house, will have to wait for future historians, for documents not yet released, diaries not yet published (if there should be any) and books not yet written. Many incidents never reached the newspapers. For example, while Prime Minister Churchill and the Duke of Windsor were both in Hyde Park in September, 1944, the President left them together in his office in the library so they could talk in private.

In spite of stringent security measures which increased greatly during the later years, "Springwood" kept its usual appearance. True, there was a small guard house at the gate and close inspection of all visitors. But the watching was discreetly done. When the President came to dinner at our house, our place was invaded in the afternoon for a careful check-up. Several hours before he arrived, guards were posted around the house, in the cellar and on the top floor. Flood lights were set up. When he arrived, he brought the usual quota of State police and secret service men with him. But once he was there, the guards were unobtrusive; they faded into the landscape. One day, having arrived early at the Poughkeepsie station to meet a friend, I was lying on the grass dozing in the sun. On looking up, I saw the blue Ford drawn up with other cars waiting in front of the station. Only when I got up to talk to the President and Princess Martha, who had come to meet her husband, the Crown Prince of Norway, was I aware of the watchful eyes of Colonel Starling and the secret service guards. They were very much there, but very much in the background. I tell this because it shows the simplicity of F.D.R.'s

life at Hyde Park. He behaved as would anyone else going to meet a friend at the station. Sometimes he would by-pass secretaries and put in a local call himself. Then, on answering the telephone, you might hear, "This is Franklin Roosevelt." His was a simplicity of manner that was not put on. He took the trappings of the job as a matter of course, and so easily, that they were, in effect, unobtrusive.

CLOTHES CLOSET NEXT TO F.D.R.'S HYDE PARK BEDROOM, WITH HIS WELL KNOWN NAVAL CAPE IN EVIDENCE. THESE CLOTHES WERE LEFT HERE ACCORDING TO HIS WISH.

All his life he had lived here in a certain way. He wanted that way changed as little as was humanly possible. In spite of the importance of the drama that was going on; in spite of the inevitable retinue of guards, secretaries, officials and reporters; in spite of the final addition of the library building to the grounds; the look and the feel of the place changed remarkably little.

"One stepped out of long French windows from the living-room-library and onto a green lawn. Many times in summer, when I would be told that 'the family was on the lawn,' I approached the library and saw through the open door an unforgettable picture . . . The scene was like a Currier and Ives print of life along the Hudson . . .

"In summer and holiday time the children were at home. There were boys rushing all over the place, riding ponies, practicing hurdle jumps, swinging baseball bats and tennis racquets, filling the air with their shouting . . .

"Large companies would sit down to lunch . . . Roosevelt would be at the head of the table talking to everybody, bantering with his children, teasing them and they him . . . Roosevelt played with his children as though he were one of them; he relished the practical joke of the moment as much as they did."

From "The Roosevelt I Knew," by Frances Perkins.

This was the President's favorite view, which he could see from his bedroom windows. On clear days when visibility was good he could see the Poughkeepsie bridge built in 1888 and the Mid-Hudson bridge dedicated in 1930 by him while he was Governor.

Below he is seen in his old gray sweater, having breakfast in bed and surrounded by newspapers and dispatches.

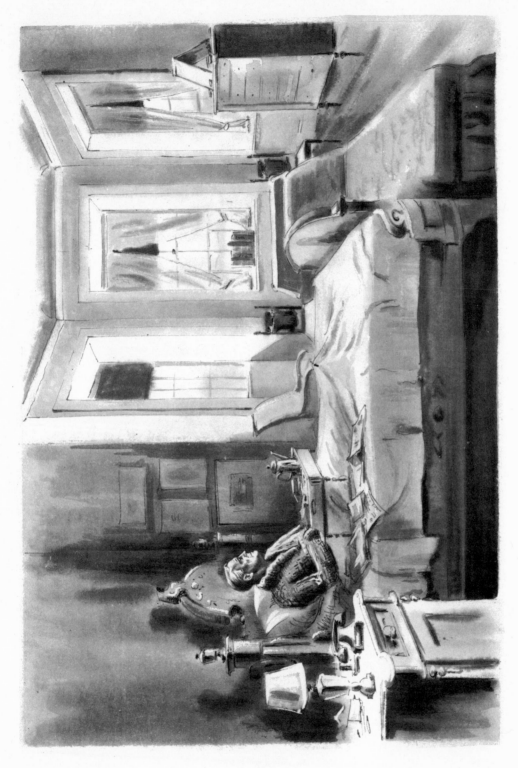

From his west bedroom window President Roosevelt could look out on one of his apple orchards in bloom, against the background of the Hudson and the hills beyond.

Below, the house on an early June morning, with Charles Van Curan, who is the second oldest employee on the Roosevelt place, sweeping the front steps, watering the plants and raking the turn-around.

123

The central ornament on the mantelpiece in F.D.R.'s bedroom is this Democratic donkey by George Ehrlich. It was a present from an English-woman to an American official whose initials are B.V.C. The sculptor (then a refugee in London) was commissioned to make a donkey with his ears laid back and his hind foot ready to deliver a swift kick. An amusing story about this donkey is revealed in this excerpt from the letter of the American naval officer who brought the statuette across the Atlantic:

"I got the donkey to the White House, practically into B.V.C.'s possession, but I was sidetracked. When I went to call on F.D.R. and Mrs., after a very nice talk with them, the box of souvenirs — stamps for F.D.R., sealskin for Mrs., etc. — was brought in. The donkey was brought in, too. I could have saved the day by telling them it was for B.V.C., but I weakened, since F.D.R. took a fancy to it at once. The result is that your donkey now adorns F.D.R.'s bedroom along with the sealskin, etc. The terrible thing is they don't know it was yours and intended for someone else."

*   *   *

In one of President Roosevelt's memorable speeches in the 1944 campaign he said: "The Republican leaders have not been content to make personal attacks upon me — or my wife — or my sons — they now include my little dog Fala."

Whelped April 7, 1940, Fala, when four months old, was brought "on approval" to "Springwood" by Miss Margaret Suckley. As a frightened newcomer to the boisterous Roosevelt household, he spent most of his first two days there under the Washington desk in F.D.R.'s small study. However, he pleased everyone immediately. But before he was formally presented to the President in the White House, at the advanced age of eight months, he went through his basic training under the supervision of Miss Suckley, with three weeks in New York City and at least four walks a day in traffic.

Taken for his first trip on the heavy cruiser *Tuscaloosa*, from then on he accompanied the President always, except when he went to Europe. He was one of F.D.R.'s favorite pets. Fala was present at the Atlantic Charter meeting. By this time he had lost his inferiority complex and had achieved a bold and successful social manner. Yet he was lost in the shuffle of this great meeting, and only at the last moment, when his master saw him moping in a corner and called to him to come and get in the final photograph, did he cheer up and happy again to be in the center of things, sit down between the President's legs, his black face wreathed in his most photogenic smile.

Fala, having his own biography, his own special alcove in the library, and his own feature movie, is so celebrated a character that his life needs no further comment from me.

Here we have two views of the Hyde Park town hall, where Franklin Roosevelt had always voted since he was twenty-one. Above is the 1891 building as you see it from the street. On the next page the President, on his son James' arm, is seen on his way to the voting booth.

Mr. Roosevelt, in a radio address from his Hyde Park home on election eve in 1940, said: "The right to place men in office, at definite, fixed dates of election for a specific time, is the right which will keep a free people always free . . .

"We have more faith in the collective opinion of all Americans than in the individual opinions of any one American.

"Your will is a part of the great will of America. Your voice is a part of the great voice of America. And when you and I stand in line tomorrow for our turn at the polls, we are voting equals . . .

"But our obligation to our country does not end with the casting of our votes.

"Every one of us has a continuing responsibility for the government which we chose.

"Democracy is not just a word, to be shouted at political rallies and then put back into the dictionary after election day.

"The service of democracy must be something more than mere lip-service.

"It is a living thing — a human thing — compounded of brains and muscles and heart and soul. The service of democracy is the birthright of every citizen, the white and the colored; the Protestant, the Catholic, the Jew, the sons and daughters of every country in the world, who make up the people of this land. Democracy is every man and woman who loves freedom and serves the cause of freedom."

As in the case of so many of the Roosevelt parties, election night was informal and exciting. There were always hordes of people of all kinds, and much running to and fro, the greatest activity concentrating around the dining-room where F.D.R. sat at the table in his shirt-sleeves, with telephones and papers on the table and friends around, with people coming in and out with messages. When his election was assured, a torchlight parade would start from the village and walk up the drive. All the family and friends would swarm out on the front porch, and F.D.R. would say a few words to the cheering and waving group on the lawn and the turn-around.

Among the informal remarks to torchlight paraders at Hyde Park on election night of 1940, the President said: "I claim to remember it, but the family say that I do not, and that was the first election of Grover Cleveland in 1884. I was one-and-a-half years old at that time and I remember the torchlight parade that came down here that night — as they say, 'Believe it or not.'

"And this youngster here, Franklin Jr., was just saying to me that he wondered whether Franklin Third, who is up there in that room, will also remember tonight. He also is one-and-a-half years old."

Or again, on the same occasion, four years later, he returned to the same subject: "I remember my first torch-light parade right here in 1892, Cleveland's election, and I was asleep, or supposedly asleep, right up in this window, a little room at the head of the stairs, and I was listening, and I didn't know what was the matter; a queer light outside the window, with people coming up on farm wagons; before the days of the automobile. It was Hyde Park, a large part of it, coming down here to have a Democratic celebration.

"And I got up and appeared down here in an old-fashioned nightgown of some kind, on this porch, and I was wrapped in an old buffalo robe that came out of a wagon, and I had a perfectly grand evening."

LENOX CHINA DESIGNED FROM SUGGESTIONS MADE BY
THE PRESIDENT, INCORPORATING THE THREE FEATHERS
AND ROSES OF THE ROOSEVELT FAMILY CREST.

129

An unusual feature of "Springwood" is this railroad siding, where coal and other freight for the place was sidetracked. During his Presidency, not only his own private car stopped here, but also Winston Churchill's and Queen Wilhelmina's. F.D.R. was glad to receive them in this informal way, because it gave him the opportunity to show them, on the drive up the hill, his beloved primeval forest.

It was here one day that the President was driving Arthur Krock of *The New York Times*, when a train passed and the engineer, recognizing the President, blew his whistle and waved. F.D.R. waved back and, turning to Krock, said: "An old friend; we always wave when we see each other." At the end of the train a hobo was riding the rods; he, too, recognized the President and waved from his precarious perch. The *Times* writer asked: "Is he your friend?" "Yes," said the President, laughing and waving: "He is my friend, too!"

President Roosevelt's funeral train came to this siding, and his body was carried on a caisson up the hill, through the forest, to the rose garden where he is buried.

We have already seen this white birch grove in the picture of "Val-Kill Cottage." Here we look west across the pond to the dirt road that goes from "Top Cottage" to the "Val-Kill" stone gateposts on Route 9-G. Directly across the state road is the Moses Smith farm. The outdoor fireplace built of fieldstone shows at the right of the picture.

"Father, after he became President, was always accompanied on his visits to Hyde Park by members of the press. Many times mother and father would invite them to picnic lunches or supper cooked out of doors over the grill at 'Val-Kill.' Often father would sit there with the correspondents gathered around him on benches or on the grass, while he carried on very informal and strictly 'off-the-record' discussions."

From a letter by Mrs. John Boettiger, daughter of F.D.R.

* * *

As I have already noted, the President took the greatest interest in, and his taste exerted a strong influence on, those public buildings erected locally under the various work programs of his administration. The new schools in Hyde Park were among the many throughout the country which benefited from P.W.A. grants. The Public Buildings Administration erected new post offices in Dutchess County, first in Poughkeepsie and in Rhinebeck, later at Hyde Park and Wappingers Falls. These post offices were all copied from old buildings in their respective townships, buildings which had disappeared with the years.

In the big library of his home, we see the President in 1939, studying blueprints and discussing plans for the Roosevelt High School with the Hyde Park board of education.

"These new schools symbolize, I think, two modern government functions in this country of ours, each of which is proving itself more and more vital to the continuance of our democracy," the President said at the dedication of three schools in Hyde Park on October 5, 1940.

"One of them is the old function, based on the ideal and the understanding of the founding fathers, that true democratic government cannot long endure in the midst of widespread ignorance. They recognized that democratic government would call for the intelligent participation of all its people, as enlightened citizens, citizens equipped with what we used to call in the old days 'a schooling.' From this time to our own, it has always been recognized as a responsibility of government, that every child have the right to a free and liberal education . . .

"Tyranny hates and fears nothing more than the free exchange of ideas, the free play of the mind that comes from education . . .

"Finally, we are all happy that the trustees, with rare foresight, have secured adequate acreage for the schools, enough for expansion in the century to come, that I have spoken of. Every boy and girl in these schools will have elbow room, plenty of space and plenty of air for sports and games and recreation of all kinds. The next generation will not have to worry about buying more athletic fields, or about the high cost of adjoining property."

＊　＊　＊

I should like to digress for a moment, to discuss our local architecture and its relation to the community. Much fine building was done in the early and middle years of the past century. You have seen St. James Church and chapel and the Hyde Park town hall already. In the country many of the sturdily built but neglected Victorian farmhouses are now being bought and done over. They are very desirable. But the large estates are not. During the latter half of the past century the large country places underwent great changes. The scale of the few Eighteenth-century houses, and the not too grandiose comfort of the Victorian ones, like James Roosevelt's, was not sufficiently impressive for the taste or the pocketbooks of the later Nineteenth-century landowners. New houses were built, old ones were destroyed, added to, or remodeled, in the eclectic manner of Hunt, McKim, Mead and White, and other well known architects. The children who inherited these mansions found them a burden, for the continual devaluation of the dollar's purchasing power reduced the incomes that made the upkeep of such estates possible. Moreover, the countryside was not especially fashionable, the people far from gregarious. There were no country clubs. It was too far from New York for commuting. These factors have influenced the most marked changes — the

133

transformation of many of the large estates into schools and various other public or semi-public institutions.

President Roosevelt, more than any other contemporary statesman, directed those deep forces which, in this as well as other communities, have changed many of our institutional buildings. Here, our high schools have become large, handsome, and more efficient buildings, while the great estates have been either eliminated, or are in the process of being reduced to family size.

*   *   *

From Benjamin Haviland's barns and cross his pond you get an interesting view of the Franklin D. Roosevelt High School. Uncle Ben sold the site to the Hyde Park board of education. F.D.R. suggested that the school be called the Haviland School, but the board thought otherwise.

THE HYDE PARK POST OFFICE.

During the years in which I was working on the murals for the Rhinebeck and Hyde Park post offices, President Roosevelt gave me many preliminary suggestions, and visited my studio several times while the murals were under way. This is another example of his interest in Dutchess County history, evident also in his suggestions to Gerald Foster, who painted some of the murals in the Poughkeepsie post office, and to Henry Billings, who did those in Wappingers Falls. As the Rhinebeck murals dealt with the Eighteenth-century, F.D.R. wanted Hyde Park to emphasize the Nineteenth. He thought there ought to be at least one panel on the Bards (I did three), one on the Stoutenberghs, a view of the Union Corners race track, the Dickinson mill, and the Crum Elbow meeting house. The panel in which he took most interest, however, showed his Uncle John and Jacob Buckhout discussing the ice boat *Icicle*. You will see these subjects in the following sketches from my murals for the Hyde Park post office. Mr. Roosevelt sent me, for information, to some of the old-timers in the village, and suggested other source material. He later checked a list of possible subjects. When the inch-scale model of the murals was ready, he motored up and pointed out mistakes in the rigging and action of the ice boats. One night when he came to dinner, I showed him the cartoons where these errors had been corrected.

135

That night he also quizzed me about a peculiar looking boat, a hay boat, with which he wasn't familiar. He was quite satisfied, however, with my historical sources authenticating its appearance. I painted F.D.R. in three of the nineteen panels. In one he is seen chopping dead wood from a reforestation lot; in another he discusses the plans for the new high school with the Hyde Park board of education; and in the third he entertains the King and Queen of England at "Top Cottage."

"When we came to the problem of Hyde Park," the President said in his informal remarks at the laying of the Hyde Park post office cornerstone, on November 6, 1940, "we tried very hard to get a picture of the old Stoutenbergh homestead that stood within the memory of some people now living over here on the brow of the hill . . . But we could not get a real picture of what it looked like . . . We did find, however, a pen-and-ink sketch . . . of the original old John Bard house that stood, as far as we can make out, about halfway between St. James Church and the Vanderbilt barn. It was a very interesting sketch, because it showed not merely the ground plan and the elevation of a building that looked just like this — except it was of wood — but it also showed the roof plan, and the roof of this building is quite unique

"The Bard home was built, as I remember the date, about 1760, and the roof line is found only in two or three other buildings in this country . . .

136

As you know, the Bard place up here is probably the oldest estate in the north that has been kept as an estate for nearly two hundred years and under most careful supervision and care. Thereby we commemorate not merely the fact that John Bard was the grandson of the original patentee of the land north of the creek and called it Hyde Park in honor of the Hyde family . . . but also because he was a very great naturalist."

Jacob E. Buckhout discusses the *Icicle* with its owner, John Roosevelt, while Archibald Rogers joins them. As you will remember, these three men were the local leaders of the sport in the Eighteen-eighties. Quite apart from his interest in iceboating itself, young Franklin obviously enjoyed his association with them. In the middle ground, his lateen-rigged *Hawk* is just starting out, and the Rogers' *Jack Frost* is taking a sharp tack on one runner.

Dr. John Bard, friend of Benjamin Franklin and member of his club, was the first president of the New York Medical Society; he, with Dr. Peter Middleton, performed the first dissection for instruction and the first diagnosis of, and successful operation for, extra uterine pregnancy recorded in the colonies. He was virtually public-health officer of New York City, fought yellow fever, and recommended the purchase of Bedloe's Island for a quarantine station. His son, Dr. Samuel, was instrumental in founding the medical school of King's College, later the College of Physicians and Surgeons of Columbia University; was its first professor of medicine and its first president. He was also the first to agitate for a hospital. Although loyalists in the Revolution, the Bards were highly respected by both sides, Dr. Samuel taking care of President Washington in 1788, with Dr. John as consultant. They were also great farmers; Samuel Bard was the first president of the Society of Dutchess County for the Promotion of Agriculture, in 1806. The Bards brought over

merino sheep to improve local breeds; encouraged the use of clover as a crop; experimented with Italian melons, which they are seen discussing in the mural, and were among the first to use gypsum as fertilizer. Considering the achievements of these men, it is a pity that two so great physicians and scientists have been very nearly forgotten.

✻   ✻   ✻

Old Hyde Park records mention many fires. The panel above shows Dr. Samuel Bard giving first aid at a neighbor's fire. His son William holds the lantern and his son-in-law, John McVickar, supports the wounded man. The latter was rector of St. James Church, the first professor of political philosophy (economics) at King's College (now Columbia University), and author of a biography of his father-in-law which I found most readable. The experiments and the versatile lives of these Eighteenth-century Americans, who were men in the tradition of Jefferson, had an undoubted effect on F.D.R.

139

The President had told me about the Quaker colony and the Crum Elbow meeting house, built about 1797. It is tucked away back of the hills "out east." At the time depicted here, 1820, it served an active congregation; it now remains a well preserved but rarely used white clapboard building.

*   *   *

The first settlers in Hyde Park, sometime before 1741, were Jacobus Stoutenbergh and his wife, Margaret Teller. In the mural we see him, with his sons and slaves, clearing the land. His log cabin was the first house in the village. The King's Highway, our present Route 9, then a grassy "waggon" road, passed in front of his cabin door.

*   *   *

The Dickinson grist and saw mill, built before 1797 by Dr. John Bard, is the only surviving home of early Hyde Park industry. When I drew it for this mural it was still used for a feed and lumber warehouse. Young Franklin Roosevelt knew it as a functioning saw mill and the site of a prosperous business.

F.D.R.'s interest in ships sharpened his awareness of the River's active life from the earliest days. On the site of what is now the New York Central railroad station, Richard de Cantillon, a Stoutenbergh son-in-law, had his landing. His West India trading packets sailed from here with lumber or wheat, and returned with rum and molasses. It is not unlikely that the  great-great-great-grandchildren of the fishermen who are seen mending nets supplied shad, during the season, to the Roosevelts. A hay boat is being loaded from the wagon near the dock warehouse. At the far right of the mural you can see the *Clermont* steaming up the Hudson.

142

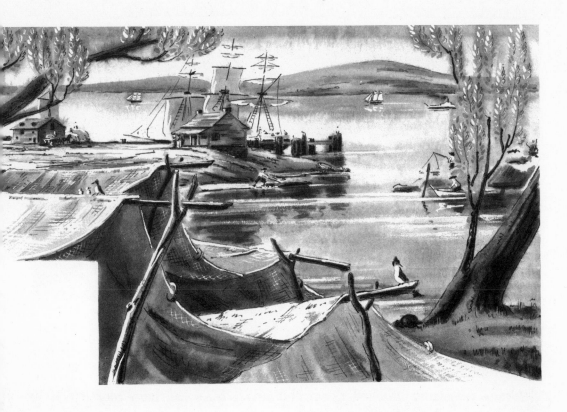

Although young Franklin did not know the Union Corners race track himself, he remembered his father's talking about it. Presumably it was the scene of some of Gloster's triumphs. You may recall that Gloster was James Roosevelt's champion trotting horse. Anyway, it was important enough to the President to want a mural on the subject. In the panel, James Roosevelt, in the Eighteen-fifties, is seen talking to a friend from his breaking cart. Daniel Wigg, a local racing celebrity, trots by, watched from the other side of the fence by Martin Van Buren, living then in Columbia County, and James K. Paulding, his former secretary of the Navy, popular novelist, and resident of Hyde Park. The refreshment wagon in the foreground contains yellow cans and a bottle of Daniel Wigg's "Whirlbone Liniment," equally good for man and beast. When I was a boy, this liniment was still used in the neighboring stables.

This is the last mural panel shown in this book. The other subjects relating to the history of Hyde Park are less intimately connected with President Roosevelt.

"'Hello, Henry, come down from your perch and introduce me to your missus; mine couldn't come with me, she's up in Campo looking after the children.' As Henry climbed down the ladder from the barn roof which he was repairing," Mrs. Henry Morgenthau, Jr., writes, "his 'Missus' came out, attracted by the friendly, booming voice, and laughter, and saw a tall, slim, incredibly handsome man. Now thirty-three years have gone by, but that first encounter is still vivid, because the man was Franklin Roosevelt. It was always that way when he came to "Fishkill Farms"; first as a comparatively carefree young man, and at the end an over-burdened, war-weary commander-in-chief. At our farm he seemed to relax, and before he reached the door we heard the familiar shout and knew that the Roosevelt family had come to call on the Morgenthaus.

"In the early days these visits sometimes came at unusual hours. Late one very cold December night, we were trying to keep the old furnace going in our farmhouse, when a car stopped at the door and three frozen men got out; the fourth sat behind the wheel of his car. He was blue with cold, but his voice was louder and cheerier than ever as he said, 'Henry, get me out of here; we are all starved and frozen.' He was then chairman of the Taconic Park Commission, but, not content to sit at home and study maps, he himself drove the engineers over the mountains, following only wood trails to find how the parkway should eventually be laid out.

"When he left to go home that night, he said: 'This was grand. I'm warm as toast, and I'll go home now. This is the 'Half-way House,' and I can stop here every time I explore the countryside.' But the engineers with him confided to us they hoped there would be no more of these perilous trips.

"When F.D.R. was Governor we built our present home. 'The Homestead,' as we like to call it, continued to be visited often by the Franklin Roosevelt family, and always with the same informality. It seemed as if here he could throw off the burdens of state and nation and discuss local affairs, and just be himself. He loved to talk about the country and his neighbors, and he wanted the press, who were assigned to him, to see other parts of his beloved Dutchess County, and so we hit upon the idea of an annual clam bake, as traditional to the farmer in Dutchess County as the Holstein cow and cider in the autumn. This was F.D.R.'s party, to which he brought all his family, his house guests, and the newspaper men and their wives. There were about one hundred of us altogether. Usually we had the bake in the fall, with the big oak watching over us, a harvest moon overhead, and a huge bonfire to keep us warm. The President loved to sing the old, familiar tunes. He used to say, 'I like melody, but I hate jazz,' so Hughey came from New York with several of his musicians who played the banjo, guitar, and drum, and all of us joined in the singing. Then there always had to be a special little group which included Fred Storm of the United Press, Marvin MacIntyre, Henry Morgenthau, Jr., and the tenor, F.D.R., himself. They sang 'Home on the Range,' etc., and ended with a song which the President insisted was well known when he was a boy but which none of the rest of us had ever heard. 'How clear is the air — I wonder what's in it. Wocky Doodle, Wocky Doodle, Wocky Doodle, I A.' When he finished that song, we knew that the President had shed all of his cares and was completely relaxed.

"After the clam bake was over we went into the house to our living room (F.D.R. always called it our 'best parlor') and danced, ending with the

145

Virginia reel led by Eleanor Roosevelt and the host. F.D.R. sat in a comfortable armchair, clapping in rhythm to the dancers, and calling the figures. He seemed to thoroughly enjoy every bit of it and if the thought was ever in the back of his mind, 'I once was pretty good at this myself,' his serene expression never betrayed him."

Miss Laura Delano, one of F.D.R.'s first cousins, lives some seven miles north of "Springwood." She is mentioned frequently in his early letters. As President, he visited her often, and enjoyed bringing his guests there. On summer evenings her terrace is cool and quiet, a very agreeable place to sit and look at the sweeping view of the river and the mountains.

I remember one night at dinner, at this house, when F.D.R. had just come from Washington, from sweltering heat and international crisis. He looked tired. But after one cocktail, a good dinner, and three hours talking to the friends there (he did most of the talking that night), he went home at eleven completely rested. It showed how much he enjoyed talking, and how much the give-and-take of conversation relaxed him.

The following anecdote as told by Colonel Starling (head of the President's secret service) to Thomas Sugrue, gives the mood of one of F.D.R.'s drives around the back roads of the country in his blue Ford.

"One afternoon at Hyde Park he ordered the small car which was fitted so that he could drive it, and with his secretaries, Miss LeHand and Miss Tully, started out for a ride. He headed for the woods between the residence and the Hudson River. Members of the detail were behind him in the big secret-service car, and behind them were State troopers in one of their automobiles. I remained at the house to answer the telephone and take care of some callers who were scheduled for the afternoon.

"When he was well into the woods the President decided to turn around and come back. He soon had his car facing the other way, but the road was narrow and the other two vehicles were temporarily stuck. Gleefully the President raced by them, and in a few minutes rolled up to the residence and called out to me: " 'Ed,' he said, looking very serious, 'I have lost the secret-service boys. I cannot find them anywhere. Do you know where they are?'

"I kept a straight face and went to the telephone. Calling the front gate, I left word for the boys that the President was waiting for them at the house. As I returned, the State troopers' car came around the corner on two wheels. Behind it was the secret-service car, also traveling at top speed. After telling them that he was sorry, and that he hoped they would not get lost again, the President drove off, a mischievous grin on his face."

From "Starling of the White House."

"Steen Valetje" ("Little Stone Valley," in Dutch), is important in F.D.R.'s story as another family house, about fifteen miles north of Hyde Park. It was the home of his maternal uncle, Warren Delano III, of his first cousins — Lyman (his junior by one year), Ellen, Laura, Jean, and Sarah, whose names are found in the letters. The three last named are sometimes referred to there as "the babies." Here, in the great rambling house, built in the middle of the past century, and lavishly decorated by Italian workmen imported for that purpose, the Delanos were brought up to a healthy country life very similar to F.D.R.'s own, with red setters and Norwegian ponies figuring largely in it. I remember Mr. Delano's courtly and distinguished presence, and Mrs. Delano's very large, friendly one, at church on Sunday in Rhinebeck. I can see her, in huge, billowing skirts, going out to her basket phaeton, with its white, fringed top, and drawn by piebald Norwegian ponies. The wide entrance drive is flanked by statuary, and I remember the dozen or more huge century plants in tubs which then used to stand in front of the long yellow brick and terra-cotta decorated house. On the whole, both inside and out, it remains almost unchanged today. This very palpable presence from another generation, in addition to his strong family feeling, gave Franklin Roosevelt much of his pleasure in this house. After his uncle and aunt died, F.D.R.'s first cousin, Lyman Delano, inherited "Steen Valetje." In the picture we see him and Mrs. Delano entertaining Queen Wilhelmina and the Netherlands foreign minister, Eelco Van Kleffens, whom the President has brought to tea.   *   *   *

"Now that it is in the papers that our guests over the week-end were Her Majesty, the Queen of the Netherlands, her daughter, their grandchildren, and various members of their household, I want to tell you one or two things about Queen Wilhelmina which I think may be of interest.

"While she sat on the grass near the swimming pool with me, watching her two little granddaughters, the Queen talked about some of the things she is thinking over in relation to the future. She said that she made it a point to see every person who came out of Holland, particularly young boys. They told her what they had been through and what they were thinking about the future, and these things helped her to have a vision of what will need to be done in her country and in the post-war world . . ."

From "My Day," by Eleanor Roosevelt, July 16, 1942.

On July 24, 1940, the President called on Justice of the Peace Steeholm at Salt Point. " 'Hardy Steeholm', the President said, as the judge tells the story, 'I came here first of all as a neighbor,' (with that inimitable pronunciation of the word which has become so exclusively identified with F.D.R.) , 'and,' — his voice dropping to a confidential tone — 'to talk a little politics'."

"The President remarked that he knew the old house well; he reminisced at some length about his own early experience in the political life of Dutchess County, and he talked of his interest in its history and its people. I congratulated him on his nomination.

" 'How do you feel about it, Hardy,' he said. (By this time, as was his custom, he called me by my first name) . 'Who was your candidate?' "

150

" 'Why, Mr. President, you were, unless you had decided not to try for it.'

" 'And, in that event, who would have been your candidate?'

" 'Justice Douglas,' I answered."

" 'He was my candidate, too,' and he added with a chuckle, 'he got one vote'."

"He then grew serious, and there was an unmistakable sincerity in his voice. 'I didn't want to run; I had to do it.' There was no further comment.

" 'Hardy,' he said, 'I came here to ask a favor of you. I told them' (with emphasis on *them*), 'that when they found someone who could swim up stream, to let me know. From the reports I have had of you, you fill the bill. I want you to be my candidate for Congress against Ham Fish.'

" 'If you asked me to run against the devil himself, I would do it. I'll do it.'

" 'Thank you,' F.D.R. said; 'we shall do everything we can to help you.'

" 'I don't know whether you realize, Mr. President, that I have lived in this district only three years.'

" 'I know that,' he said, 'it has its advantages.'

" 'Moreover, I haven't always been a Democrat, but I'm a Roosevelt Democrat.'

" 'Thank God, there are a lot of you,' he said with a smile.

" 'What is worse, I haven't always approved of your administration.'

"F.D.R. threw out his arms and roared with laughter as he exclaimed, 'Hell, neither have I!' "

FALA WITH A SUMMER HAIR CUT.

As the navy building program got under way, F.D.R. had the woods to the east of Route 9 carefully timbered, under contract. Several hundred thousand board feet were cut. The lumber helped to build small wooden craft used by the navy for coastal defense. Some of this shipbuilding was done across the Hudson, north of Hyde Park, at Kingston, New York. The President was much interested and would sometimes drive out with his mother to see what was being done. In the picture Mr. Plog is telling the President about the progress of the work.

* * *

"I have been an unusually fortunate woman," his mother wrote to F.D.R. "First I had the love and protection of your grandfather, then of your father, and in my old age you have made possible for me the interesting life that I am now leading." On September 7, 1941, Mrs. James Roosevelt died. Her grave is in the old cemetery back of St. James Church where she is buried next to her husband.

He would take his foreign visitors around the county, to visit old houses, look at especially fine views, have picnics, or call on friends and members of his family. He delighted in telling of some historic incident that had taken place at the spot they were passing, or at the house they were visiting. On one of these drives with Princess Juliana, he emphasized all the Dutch names in the county for her benefit. He enjoyed having her find some Revolutionary corner cabinets "familiar," and undoubtedly gave her a clear exposition of our school system when he drove her up to the Rhinebeck school site.

In June, 1942, he brought King George II of Greece and Crown Princess Martha of Norway to tea with my mother and a few neighbors she had invited to "Glenburn." Our house is an old one, and the small place has never been sold but has descended in the family from the original Beekman grant. This fact gave Mr. Roosevelt pleasure, and so did the look of the big room which the distinguished architect Henry Bacon designed for my grandfather. When the Roosevelt house at Hyde Park was being remodeled in 1915, F.D.R. had the fixtures in our big room copied for his front hall. You can see them in "Springwood" now.

Another home which F.D.R. sometimes visited and to which he brought his guests was "The Locusts," belonging to his childhood friends and neighbors, Mr. and Mrs. Lytle Hull. On this site, Mrs. Hull's great-grandparents had lived in an immense, gray, wood Victorian gingerbread palace, on whose piazza President Grant was photographed playing chess. When the Hulls' new blue house was finished, F.D.R. drove up one afternoon to christen it — by drinking a toast in champagne and breaking his Steuben glass in the fireplace — a scene, I imagine, unique in the annals of Presidential activities. In the Hulls' visitors' book he wrote, "Franklin D. Roosevelt, successor to President Grant at 'The Locusts,' Sept. 6, 1942."

As we have already noted Franklin Roosevelt made plans and models for a number of buildings in Hyde Park. He also made a rough sketch for the Franklin D. Roosevelt Library. While it was under construction, instead of cutting down the very ancient oak by the front terrace he had the tree repaired, braced, and cared for so that it should be good for another decade at least. As a boy, he used to swing from its lower branches.

"We know from simple deduction that these fields were cultivated by the first inhabitants of America," he said at the laying of the cornerstone of the Library, November 19, 1939, "for the oak trees in these fields were striplings three centuries ago, and grew up in open fields, as is proved to us by their widespread lower branches. Therefore, they grew in open spaces, and the only open spaces in Dutchess County were the cornfields of the Indians . . .

"Of the papers which will come to rest here, I personally attach less importance to the documents of those who have occupied high public or private office than I do to the spontaneous letters which have come to me and my family and my associates from men, from women, and from children in every part of the United States, telling me of their conditions and problems, and giving me their opinions . . ."

And again, a year and seven months later, at the dedication of the

Library, he spoke about the meaning the Library should have and the purpose it should serve.

"It seems to me that the dedication of a library is in itself an act of faith. To bring together the records of the past and to house them in buildings where they will be preserved for the use of men and women in the future, a nation must believe in three things:

"It must believe in the past.

"It must believe in the future.

"It must, above all, believe in the capacity of its own people so to learn from the past that they can gain in judgment in creating their own future."

*   *   *

During his talk at the laying of this cornerstone, F.D.R. looked up from his manuscript and said: "In the summer, with his dogs, he (F.D.R.) dug into woodchuck holes in this same field, and some of you are standing on top of those holes at this moment." Then he stared directly at a group of chairs, making their feminine sitters squirm and glance uncomfortably underneath. He continued: "Indeed, the descendants of those same woodchucks still inhabit this field, and I hope that, under the auspices of the National Archivist, they will continue to do so for all time . . ."

We see the President talking to the former director, Frederick Shipman, and Miss Margaret Suckley, in his office in the Library. He furnished this room slowly, mostly from the big house. He would drive over one day with a chair, on another with a table. The look of the room, and the history connected with each object, interested him. The large rug was a gift, at the time of the Teheran conference, from the Shah of Iran. He was delighted when he brought it home to find that it just fitted this room. The curtains were made by a Virginia Works Progress Administration project. He himself had picked up the Dutch tiles, set around the fireplace. The andirons belonged to John Adams. The Chippendale chair on which Miss Suckley is sitting was the property of Samuel Chew, Chief Justice of the Provincial Court of Pennsylvania. Chew was a friend of George Washington. Our first President certainly sat in this chair, as have almost all of the celebrated persons who visited F.D.R. here. Among the pictures hanging around the walls, many of them pictures of ships on which F.D.R. had made important trips, is a small water color showing the office of Russell & Company, the Delano family business at Canton, China, in the Nineteenth-century.

Mr. Roosevelt wrote the following memorandum in longhand, telling about the desk at which he is seated in the picture at the head of this page, and which he called: "the Washington desk." "Within a few days after November 11, 1918, President Wilson decided to go to France with the American Delegation to the Peace Conference. I was asked to arrange for ship etc.

"There were only transports available. The U.S.S. Geo. Washington was luckily in port, and was hastily refitted for the President's party. Furniture and rugs were needed for his suit and I found out that a replica of Geo. Washington's desk at Mt. Vernon was available at a New York department store. It was put in Pres. Wilson's study on board.

"On the way over, he used it for the preliminary draft of the League of Nations, and when I returned to the U.S. with him in February, he used it every day, as he did again on his 3rd and 4th trips.

"In the summer of 1919, King Albert of Belgium used it coming and going.

"Later, the Geo. Washington was put out of Commission & the furnishings were sold at auction at the N. Y. Navy Yard. I notified the White House of this sale but President and Mrs. W. put in no bid. Therefore, I bid $100 for the desk & chair & they were sent to me at Hyde Park. I have used them ever since, first in the little den in the big house & since 1941 in my room in the Library.

Franklin D. Roosevelt."

Franklin Roosevelt enjoyed jokes of all kinds. When he was President, such a wealth of humorous objects flowed in that storage became a real problem. You can see a choice assortment in the basement of the Library.

But F.D.R. kept his favorites on his desk. Like the subject of Miss Grace Tully's memorandum (from the White House, April 19, 1945) which follows, the "Missouri Mule Downs Ol' Man Depression," and a similar nut and pipe cleaner pair of birds, all are characteristic of his collecting instinct, and are in themselves delightful and humorous.

"This elephant was on President Roosevelt's desk from the very first days of 1933 until his death. The President was very fond of it, and enjoyed telling his visitors that it was much larger when it first came; but every now and then either Missy or Grace would send it to the dry cleaners. Each time it came back, it had shrunk some."

*   *   *

Among other objects of interest in the Library is this sail fish, caught by F.D.R. at Cocos Island, in the Pacific Ocean, in the Nineteen-thirties. The line broke just as the President was about to pull this great fish into the boat. Rooseveltian good luck, however, caused the line to tangle around the tail of the fish, and he landed it, anyway.

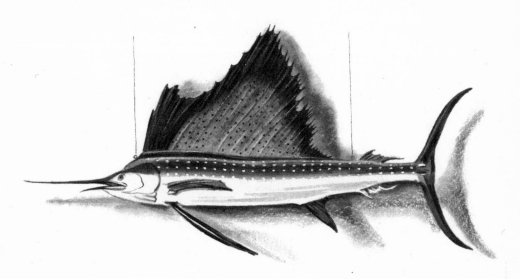

The complete set of first editions presented to the President by the author, Prime Minister Winston Churchill, take three shelves in the President's office. A lady was collecting these first editions, in order to give them to F.D.R.; Churchill, having heard about it, asked to be allowed to give them. He had all the books beautifully bound in rose morocco and tooled in gold with the Roosevelt crest. Each volume is autographed by both the President and the Prime Minister. In the last volume, "Onwards to Victory," Churchill has written on the fly leaf, "A fresh egg from the faithful hen, Quebec, 1944."

F.D.R.'s famous brown campaign hat, worn in most of the Presidential campaigns, was made by G. Sartoris, Genoa.

RAMP AND ENTRANCE TO F.D.R.'S PRIVATE OFFICE IN THE LIBRARY.

The main room of the naval collection was personally arranged by F.D.R. He sat in his chair and directed the placing of all models, prints, and pictures.

"When I was first married, I discovered that my husband was a collector," Mrs. Roosevelt says in discussing this hobby of her husband's. "I had never before come in contact with a collector. In every other aspect, he was both careful and economical. I never knew him in those early days to take a cab when he could take a street car . . . He took great care of his clothes, never spent a great deal on himself . . .

162

"As a collector he was careful too, and much of his collection was acquired at most reasonable prices, because of the fact that not many people were interested in his field when he began to collect, and his interest extended over so many years . . . His interest was in the American navy and he collected books and letters and prints and models of ships . . .

"I have often wondered why he never handed down this love of collecting to any of our children. My only explanation is that living in the house with a collector may give everyone else the feeling that only one person in a household can indulge this taste, and even then it is always a question of whether the family will have to move out in order to keep the collection intact and properly housed!

"All through the first years in Washington, I wondered where the additions to the naval collection would find a home on our return to New York, where the house seemed already full, but it was managed, and I wasted much time trying to restrain a collector which simply cannot be done."

(About their first European trip together.)

". . . but Franklin bought books, books, everywhere he went.

"His French was very good, so in Paris he did the bargaining for the books, etc., but when we reached Italy, I spoke better Italian than he did. However, after a few days he gave up taking me on expeditions to shop when he really was going to bargain, because he said he did a great deal better without me, and insisted I accepted whatever the man said and believed it to be the gospel truth, so as a bargainer I was useless. He got along with his poor Italian, made up largely from the Latin which he had learned in school."

From "This Is My Story," by Eleanor Roosevelt.

Mrs. James Roosevelt carried some of the stones in her car from the original Theodore Roosevelt house in Oyster Bay, Long Island, to Hyde Park. She wanted them incorporated into the Library walls. They were forgotten while that building was being constructed, so later the masons laid them on either side of the door of the gate lodge.

"About three o'clock in the morning F.D.R. drove to Thompson's Pond, near Pine Plains, to hear the walking chorus of swamp birds with a group of local ornithologists. As the dawn starts breaking, the first bird calls clear and pure in the silence. He is followed within moments by others, until there is a veritable chorus of hundreds, rising, wheeling, circling about, and scattering over the countryside to get food. After a half hour or so, the President suggests breakfast from the picnic baskets, and then goes home for 'a couple more hours of sleep' before he starts the day's work."

From Margaret L. Suckley's diary, May 10, 1942.

BIRDS MADE OF PIPE CLEANERS AND HAZEL NUTS.

A picnic at Silver Mountain as described by Margaret L. Suckley: "The flag was flying over the front door as F.D.R. was carried to his blue car. He asked the special guests of the day, a couple from Scotland and Senator Lee of Oklahoma, to drive with him. A black, shaggy little creature, who was destined to become well known, jumped into the car. He was Fala, a puppy of just four months on his trial week-end at Hyde Park. I was asked to take charge of him and was, therefore, one of the lucky ones to travel in the blue car.

"F.D.R., in high spirits, takes the lead, followed by the black secret-service car, a station wagon with the food, and a number of automobiles carrying the rest of the party. He motors between the gateposts that came from his great grandfather's place, "Mount Hope," along the highway to the wood-road through the estate; then, after twenty miles of Dutchess County scenery, he leads the cavalcade up a steep and stony road, out of the valley, back of Pine Plains, through bits of woodland, pastures and cultivated slopes, until suddenly, rounding a curve, a magnificent panorama unfolds.

"He stops his car at a gate for the Secret Service to take down the rails, then drives through scrubby growth to a clearing. There he stops near a gnarled old apple tree, and in a few minutes is comfortably settled on the ground. The party gathers around him on the grass. The Secret Service and F.D.R.'s bodyguard help the colored boy unpack the baskets. Thermos bottles of hot soup and coffee, pails of ice to cool the ginger ale and 'coke.' Everybody gets down to the business of eating fried chicken, sandwiches, fruit, cake, etc. The visitors sit in little groups around F.D.R., near enough to join in the conversation or simply to listen to him. They move around so that each may have his turn talking more directly with him. F.D.R. is completely relaxed, evidently enjoying himself to the full and making the most of a few hours of freedom. He eats with real pleasure. At his feet sits Fala, looking up hopefully at the large drumstick F.D.R. is negotiating by hand. Fala soon gets a bit of the skin and looks for more. Conversation flows easily. Later, a few stretch out on the grass for a nap. The hours slip away. The sun is sinking toward the distant Catskills. F.D.R. reluctantly looks at his watch.

"Secretary Wallace sleeps in the shade of a clump of bushes nearby, his hat over his face. Fala explores in the hope of striking up a rabbit or a squirrel. He makes friends with the guards, who are stationed in a wide circle. Finally, he wanders vaguely toward Mr. Wallace. When he encounters a pair of feet, his tail begins to wag. The Secretary of Agriculture is entirely unconscious, until Fala reaches his head and slips a cold nose and a warm tongue under the edge of the hat. With a loud yell, Mr. Wallace, only half awake, leaps to his feet. F.D.R. leads the general laughter that follows. Fala is terrified and rushes for cover!

"The spell of the afternoon is broken. The puppy has unconsciously given the signal for going home. F.D.R. and all his guests pull themselves back to the business of everyday life, and shortly every trace of the picnic has been cleaned up and F.D.R. is leading the train of cars on the return to Hyde Park."

Picnics are a Roosevelt institution. They are held on the front lawn at "Springwood," a short walk from "Val-Kill Cottage"; in the open field next to "Top Cottage," and, of course, best of all are those that entail a long drive to some distant view or especially fine spot in the woods. Anywhere to be outdoors in the fresh air. The Roosevelts have always entertained friends and even celebrated birthdays that way.

*   *   *

On one of John's birthdays a cable was handed to F.D.R.: "Arrived Paris after a delightful flight from London. Hope you are having a pleasant picnic. Mother." With a chuckle, F.D.R. promptly scribbled an answer: "Lovely picnic. Don't do it again. Franklin."

The telegram illustrated is a memento of one of the Roosevelt family picnics. It is also a memento of one of numerous visits paid to the Roosevelts at Hyde Park by both reigning and refugee royalty; as well as a charming example of F.D.R.'s warm personal touch in even quite formal human relations.

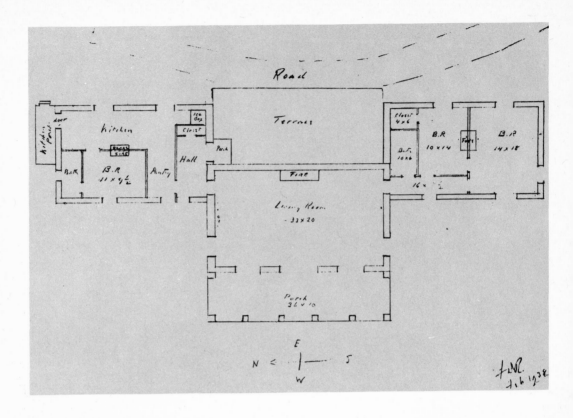

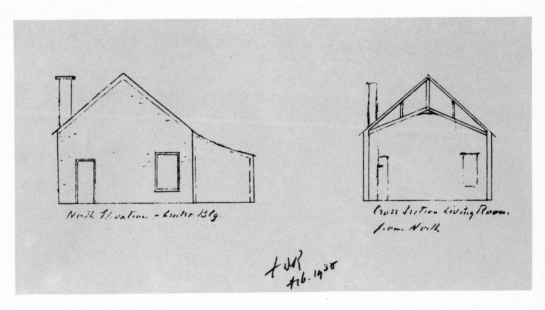

North Elevation - Center Bldg.

Cross Section Living Room from North

170

On the high ridge that runs parallel with Route 9-G, Mr. Roosevelt built the stone house which he called "Top Cottage" and which the press, much to his annoyance, called "the Dream House." You reach it by the dirt road that passes "Val-Kill." It is so high up that you see it plainly not only from Route 9-G but also from the west side of the Hudson. The President drew the plans for this building himself, and both plan and elevation are here reproduced. His sketches were translated by Henry J. Toombs into blueprints and working drawings. When the foundations were being laid out, F.D.R. sat in his car and directed just where the marking stakes were to be placed. The front of the house still has a new, and will always have an informal, look. When it was completed, in 1939, just in time for the picnic on June 12 given in honor of the King and Queen of England, it looked very unfinished, indeed. F.D.R. was enthusiastically interested in it, in its construction, in its furnishings, in its landscaping. And this was natural for "Top Cottage" was the first house that was his own.

When the King and Queen of England visited the United States in June, 1939, the President laid out the plan of their visit himself. This was a typical example of Mr. Roosevelt's attention to detail, and his pleasure in having his finger in many pies. He took particular care in planning their Hyde Park stay and the picnic which he gave for them at "Top Cottage." The President wanted as informal an atmosphere as possible; considering the circumstances, he achieved it. The press stories notwithstanding, only one small dish of hot dogs was prepared and served to the King and Queen, beside the regular lunch. This to show them what a real, live American hot dog was like. There were no press photographers. There were card tables on the porch for the twenty-eight distinguished guests, while others sat around the platform and under the trees. Before lunch, the hundred and fifty guests met the King and Queen. After lunch, two American Indians gave a song-and-dance recital. Needless to say, this was a gala event; no such thing had ever happened in the county before, and it is not likely to happen again.

Describing the visit, Mrs. Roosevelt wrote:

"Numerous details have taken up our time today. The old house has been filled with flowers by my mother-in-law's kind friends. Tho there is not the same sense of space here as in the White House, I hope that the quiet of the country will be welcome after the busy days which Their Majesties have been thru . . .

"On Sunday, we drove to church along a road which was lined with people the greater part of the way. There were masses of people in the village of Hyde Park and outside the church . . .

"After lunch, Princess Te Ata and Ish Ti Opi gave a short program. The platform was built around the trees and the setting was quite perfect for the Indian singers and legends . . .

"Nothing was planned for the afternoon, so we sat under the trees around

the swimming pool. The President and the King went in swimming, while the Queen and Lady Nunburnholme, with some other members of the household, sat around under the trees with me and looked on . . .

"A procession of cars drove down to the little Hyde Park station at 11 P.M. to see the royalty off, and a crowd was gathered in the village and at the station in spite of the fact that during dinner we had a very heavy thunderstorm . . .

"However, it was all over when we started for the station. There the King and Queen said goodbye and a word of thanks for every one. They remembered each individual . . . Once on the platform of their car, they turned to stand until the train pulled out. The crowd suddenly began to sing 'Auld Lang Syne . . .' and I am sure they (the reporters) sensed a feeling of regret, that seemed to be in every individual present, at bidding goodbye to this gracious couple who have endeared themselves to all who have seen them.

"We stood and waved, but my mother-in-law reminded us of the old superstition that one must not watch people out of sight, so before they turned the bend we were back in our cars and on our way home."

". . . Perhaps the most personal impression which remains with me is the never-failing thoughtfulness and graciousness of our guests. No one was ever forgotten, no one was ever greeted except with a smile, and everyone was greeted.

"At Hyde Park, the servants we brought from Washington suffered from a jinx which followed its course in three mishaps: My mother-in-law's serving table in the dining room has a center standard. Too many dishes were put on one side, and in the middle of the dinner the table tipped over. No one could think for a minute because of the noise of breaking china.

"Later in the evening, with a tray full of glasses, water, ginger ale and bottles, one of our men going into the big library slipped and dropped the entire tray on the floor. And as a final catastrophe, on Sunday afternoon, my husband, moving backwards across the grass by the swimming pool, almost sat on another tray of glasses and pop bottles . . ."

From "My Day," by Eleanor Roosevelt.

174

"The Prime Minister of Great Britain, with his daughter, has been visiting the President and Mrs. Roosevelt at Hyde Park for three days and, he has now returned to Quebec." This report, necessarily meager, due to war-time security, appeared in *The New York Times* on August 16, 1943. The Prime Minister's two other war-time visits to the United States were treated with equal restraint by the press. It was quite a contrast to the detailed stories describing the visit of the King and Queen of England, only four years before.

Mr. Roosevelt always liked a simple way of living. Here at "Top Cottage," and at other Presidential retreats, he wanted to be "away from the show." He insisted on informality. "Top Cottage" reflected this personal attitude. It even grew rather informally, for at first it was only to be on one floor. Later, when the need for more rooms became apparent, F.D.R. had bedrooms and baths added in the attics under the Dutch roof to which he was so partial. Much of the furniture belonged to Mrs. Roosevelt's grandmother, and the President brought it down from her Tivoli house. At "Top Cottage," Mr. Roosevelt kept his books on nature, on the land, birds, animals, explorations, and also particular personal gifts. Meals were usually served on card tables.

You get a sense of this informal atmosphere in the picture of the porch, where Harry Hopkins and Miss Grace Tully play cards, Prime Minister Churchill reads, and F.D.R. chats with Mrs. Averell Harriman. The personal and historic implications of such scenes will undoubtedly become available later. It is reasonable to suppose, however, that preliminary discussions and even vital decisions were reached here.

The same atmosphere of "Top Cottage" informality is suggested in this entry for October 11, 1943, from Miss Suckley's diary: "General Eisenhower's aide de camp, General Bedell Smith, came to see F.D.R. They were closeted together for long periods.

"Mrs. Roosevelt took a picnic lunch to the 'Hilltop Cottage'—just seven of us seated before the fire at two card tables. Ethel (Roosevelt) and I 'discovered' there was just enough coffee left in the thermos for the President at the end of the meal, I took it to the pantry so no one else would drink it. Finally . . . The President asked for his coffee; I went out, heated it up, brought it back, poured it and put the cup at his right. He and the General were immersed in conversation. The President said, 'Won't you have some coffee, General?' 'Yes, sir, thank you,' and drank the President's coffee!"

Immortalized in important war correspondence between Hopkins and Roosevelt are Hyde Park people connected with the President, some of whom appear in the pages of this book. Robert E. Sherwood in "Roosevelt and Hopkins" writes: "Roosevelt and Hopkins also contrived some code names for their own private use in cables — as follows: Marshall was 'Plog'; King, 'Barrett'; Eisenhower, 'Keuren'; Spaatz, 'Depew'; Clark, 'Robert'; Stark, 'Draiss'; Churchill, 'Moses Smith'; 'Cripps, 'Mrs. Johansen'; Portal, 'Rev. Wilson'; Brooke, 'Mr. Bee'."

"Every one of these code names represented was taken from Hyde Park. Grace Tully has told me that William Plog was Mrs. James Roosevelt's super-intendent for many years (he always called the President "Mr. Franklin"), Depew was her chauffeur, Robert McGauhey was her butler and, as this is writ-ten, is still at Hyde Park. Moses Smith rented a farm on the place and was the moving spirit of the Franklin D. Roosevelt Home Club. Reverend Wilson was Rector of St. James Church, Christian Bee caretaker of Roosevelt's hilltop cot-tage, Barrett ran the farm, Van Curan (misspelled by Hopkins) worked with Plog, Draiss worked on roads and trees, Mrs. Johansen was a neighbor who ran a gas station and restaurant near Mrs. Roosevelt's cottage."

Sitting on the porch of "Top Cottage," Mr. Roosevelt could overlook his land, through vistas he'd cut from the woods that covered this hill. He could easily see the Franklin D. Roosevelt High School north of his own boundary line. Directly below him, but hidden by the trees, was "Val-Kill," the fieldstone cottage and the swimming pool he'd built. Here and there he would recognize plantations of trees. Between 9-G, which stood out as does

the road on a map, and the old State road, lay natural woodlands and the fields of his mother's acres. He could imagine himself riding with his children over the wood road that connected the land of "Val-Kill" with the old home in which he had been brought up. He knew just where the house was, though he could not see it. Trees hid it as they did his half-brother's house to the south or the Newbold house to the north. But they all held memories; they were still a part of his life. Family and friends were living there. He knew just how the dirt road, beyond "Springwood," eased over the ridge and kept going gently down until it reached the Hudson. What he could see and what he remembered was backdropped against the flowing River and the Catskills.

The two houses, "Top Cottage" and "Springwood," as well as the land itself,

178

have significance, as a great President's background. But they are much more than that, much more than merely Mr. Roosevelt's country background. They were an integral part of his life. As "Springwood" touched the intimate memories of his past, so "Top Cottage" held the peaceful promise of his future. It was the retreat to which he would go when his terms of office were over. Here he could do all the things he had wanted to do "as a private citizen"; work on his papers in the Library and write the history of those decades he had so profoundly influenced by his leadership and by his eloquence.

But that was not to be. Three weeks and five days after his return from the Yalta Conference, President Roosevelt went for an extended rest to his cottage in Warm Springs, Georgia. There on April 12, 1945, he died suddenly.

Where the forest touches the River, Franklin Roosevelt was brought on his last journey. There, at the private railroad siding, he came on the same train, manned with the same crew, which had carried him through the then recent political campaign. The flag-draped coffin was guarded by veterans of the war he had led. It was borne up the hill, through the primeval forest, on a rattling caisson. A black-draped horse followed. Twenty-one guns at slow intervals boomed; a military band played a dirge; planes flew above. In the rose garden at the top, his body was met by some of the men and women with whom he had worked for victory — by a few friends and neighbors — by the people who worked on his place — and by his family. The soldiers who stood at attention around the hemlock hedge also stood for the millions to whom Franklin Roosevelt was and is a living symbol.

At the dedication of the place a year after the President's death, Mrs. Roosevelt said: "He always felt that this was his home, and he loved the house and the view, the woods, special trees, the particular spots where he played as a child; or where he had ridden his horse as a boy and a man, or where he later drove his car when he was no longer able to ride.

"Life here had always a healing quality for him. Here he spent the summer nine months after he had infantile paralysis, and laboriously worked to regain some measure of strength which would enable him to get about. As he gained physically, the healing of the spirit went forward at the same time . . .

"My husband's spirit will live in this house, in the Library and in the quiet garden inside the hedge where he wished his body to lie. It is his life and his character and his personality which will live with us and which will endure and be imparted to those who come to see the surroundings in which he grew to maturity.

"It is with pleasure that our children and I see this house dedicated to the people and opened to them. It was the people, all of the people of this country and of the world, whom my husband loved and kept constantly in his mind and heart. He would want them to enjoy themselves in these surroundings, and to draw from them rest and peace and strength, as he did all the days of his life."

On December 26, 1937, in a memorandum written to his son James, Mr. Roosevelt told him just how and where he wished to be buried. So, even after death, he was able to exert his personal influence in the minute details of this intimate and final project:

"A plain white monument — no carving or decoration — to be placed over my grave, east and west, as follows: Length, 8 feet; width, 4 feet; height, 3 feet. Whole to be set on marble base extending 2 feet out from monument all around — but said base to be no more than 6 inches from the ground.

"I hope that my dear wife will on her death be buried there also and that the monument contain no device or inscription except the following on the south side:

Franklin Delano Roosevelt

1882 . 19 -

Anna Eleanor Roosevelt

1884 . 19 -

"We seek peace—enduring peace—more than an end to war; we want an end to this brutal, inhuman, and thoroughly impractical method of settling the differences between Governments . . . The only limit to our realization of tomorrow will be our doubts of today. Let us move forward with strong and active faith."

*   *   *

From the undelivered Jefferson Day speech on which the President was working on the eve of his death.

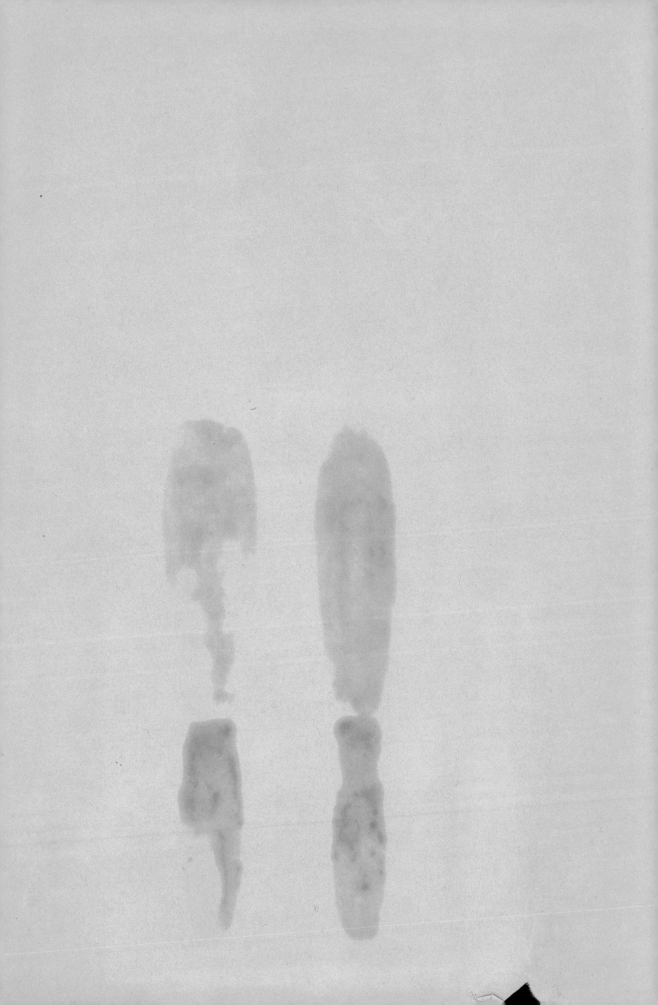